The Mother Mirror

Currents in Comparative Romance Languages and Literatures

Tamara Alvarez-Detrell and Michael G. Paulson
General Editors

Vol. 32

PETER LANG
New York • Washington, D.C./Baltimore
Bern • Frankfurt am Main • Berlin • Vienna • Paris

Laurie Corbin

The Mother Mirror

Self-Representation and
the Mother-Daughter Relation
in Colette, Simone de Beauvoir,
and Marguerite Duras

PETER LANG
New York • Washington, D.C./Baltimore
Bern • Frankfurt am Main • Berlin • Vienna • Paris

Library of Congress Cataloging-in-Publication Data

Corbin, Laurie.
The mother mirror: self-representation and the mother-daughter relation in Colette, Simone de Beauvoir, and Marguerite Duras / Laurie Corbin.
p. cm. — (Currents in comparative Romance languages and literatures; vol. 32)
Includes bibliographical references and index.
1. French literature—20th century—History and criticism.
2. Autobiography. 3. Colette, 1873–1954—Criticism and interpretation.
4. Beauvoir, Simone de, 1908– —Criticism and interpretation.
5. Duras, Marguerite—Criticism and interpretation. 6. Mothers and daughters—France. I. Title. II. Series.
PQ307.A65C65   840.9'353—dc20   95-7472
ISBN 0-8204-2743-8 (hardcover)
ISBN 0-8204-5595-4 (paperback)
ISSN 0893-5963

Die Deutsche Bibliothek-CIP-Einheitsaufnahme

Corbin, Laurie:
The mother mirror: self-representation and the mother-daughter relation in Colette, Simone de Beauvoir, and Marguerite Duras / Laurie Corbin.
– New York; Washington, D.C./Baltimore; San Francisco; Bern; Frankfurt am Main; Berlin; Vienna; Paris: Lang.
(Currents in comparative Romance languages and literatures; Vol. 32)
ISBN 0-8204-2743-8 (hardcover)
ISBN 0-8204-5595-4 (paperback)
NE: GT

Cover design by Nona Reuter.

© 1996, 2001 Peter Lang Publishing, Inc., New York

All rights reserved.
Reprint or reproduction, even partially, in all forms such as microfilm, xerography, microfiche, microcard, and offset strictly prohibited.

for my family

Acknowledgements

My sincere thanks to Elaine Marks, whose clarity of thought and expression continues to shape my thinking and writing in many ways. Comments and advice from Mary Lydon and Yvonne Ozzello have also been invaluable and I thank them for their scrupulous attention to both form and content.

I am grateful for the financial support received through a fellowship from the Wisconsin Alumni Research Foundation, the Chair's Dissertator Award from the Department of French and Italian at the University of Wisconsin, and the University League Award for Excellence in the Humanities through the Women's Studies Program at the University of Wisconsin.

Indiana University-Purdue University at Fort Wayne has been very generous in helping with publication expenses.

I thank my father, J. Wesley Corbin, for teaching me to love learning. My mother, Virginia Corbin, with her strength, generosity, and love, has been a model for me in my life and my work. I do not know how to thank my sister, Linda Corbin-Pardee, for all of the help that she has given me except to say that her wisdom and humor are a part of this book.

I gratefully acknowledge permission to quote the following works:

Simone de Beauvoir, *Mémoires d'une jeune fille rangée*, copyright © 1958 by Editions Gallimard, Paris; *Une mort très douce*, copyright © 1964 by Editions Gallimard, Paris.

Colette, *La maison de Claudine*, copyright © 1922, 1960 by Librairie Hachette, Paris; *La naissance du jour*, copyright © 1928, 1984 by Flammarion, Paris; *Sido*, copyright © 1901 by Librairie Hachette, Paris.

Marguerite Duras, *L'amant*, copyright © 1984 by Editions de Minuit, Paris; *L'amant de la Chine du Nord*, copyright © 1991 by Editions Gallimard, Paris; *Un barrage contre le Pacifique*, copyright © 1950 by Editions Gallimard, Paris.

Contents

Chapter I	Literature, Psychoanalysis, Feminism	1
Chapter II	Mourning and Jealousy in *La maison de Claudine*, *La naissance du jour*, and *Sido*	11
Chapter III	Complicity and Silence in *Mémoires d'une jeune fille rangée* and *Une mort très douce*	45
Chapter IV	Orality and Specularity in *Un barrage contre le Pacifique*, *L'Eden Cinéma*, *L'amant*, and *L'amant de la Chine du Nord*	71
Chapter V	Writing the Mother-Daughter Story: Narrative Strategies and Thematic Imagery	115
Bibliography		149
Index		167

Chapter I

Literature, Psychoanalysis, Feminism

Freud's formulation of the Oedipal triangle of father, mother, and child has not only shaped the field of psychoanalysis, it has seized the modern imagination. This troubled threesome has become increasingly central in contemporary thought. Earlier in this century the focus in literature was often on sons and mothers or on sons and fathers. More recently a greater attention is being given to the daughter's relationships with her parents. Yet, even with an ever expanding literature on the family, there is still relatively little that can be stated with certainty about these complex relationships.

The desire to examine the mother-daughter relation as it is represented in twentieth-century women's autobiographies has led me to another fascinating and troubling triad: literature, psychoanalysis, and feminism. The intersections of these three approaches to human experience have shown themselves to be almost as puzzling and provocative as the relationships structured by the family. Indeed, this threesome has been compared to the Oedipal triangle, with psychoanalysis in the paternal role, literature in the maternal role, and feminism playing the sometimes dutiful and sometimes unruly daughter.[1] Although the superimposition of these two triangles can be dangerous in that it can reduce the complexity of the constituents of each, it can be useful, at least provisionally, in explicating some of the tensions that exist in the uneasy grouping of feminism, psychoanalysis, and literature.

We must acknowledge that Freud's descriptions of family dynamics are often helpful in understanding power relations in our culture. Whether or not we agree with the manner in which the power is distributed, it is important to know how it is divided, wielded, complied with. The balance of power that structures the family in our culture is replicated throughout the culture in other relations. It is possible to see psychoanalysis as the authoritative paternal voice, literature as a maternal presence, less valued yet still with its own, different power, and feminism in between the two, sometimes relying on them and sometimes threatened.

One could ask how a feminist can work within a structure which only seems to replicate a relationship that she might have hoped to challenge, if not discard. I would suggest that we are already involved in each of these triadic structures: politics, the psyche, representation, and their conjunctions are all around us and we cannot choose to make them go away any more than we can choose against having parents. Just as Oedipus, running from his family, only found it, so a feminist will never escape her family. Similarly, the psyche is always there, as is representation. Our manners of confronting these can be very different: not every feminist is or should be a student of literature or of psychoanalytic theory. Yet it is as helpful to see the interconnections between these approaches as it is to acknowledge the ways in which we have been formed by our parents.

The Oedipal drama is useful for feminism in several ways: not only does it give us a way of seeing family passions, but it shows the hopelessness of trying to deny these passions. Both daughters and sons, even if in different ways, must confront parental power and sexuality. Both daughters and sons find that the roles of parent and child each include the roles of adversary and lover. Freud's theorizations of familial and psychological structures can be used to help make women more aware of the constraints that society and the family have imposed. Yet it is also possible to include the daughter in ways that Freud could not always envision, challenging the androcentrism that informs his work, theorizing the daughter as the subject of her own desires. This is to use Freudian thinking as descriptive yet as something more, a way of asking questions whose answers change existing structures. The enunciations of women's desires in the last century have begun to reshape both social institutions and the often unconscious motivations, assumptions, and beliefs on which these institutions are founded. When women ask themselves what they want their answers transform society in its practices and its theories.

The relationship between feminism and literature is also not without its problems although they are different from the problems of feminism and psychoanalysis. Feminism's wariness of psychoanalysis is often caused by the daughter's fear that she will either be dominated or effaced by this paternal authority. A feminist critique of literature would perhaps be founded on the daughter's worry that literature might be ineffectual, unable to affect the problems that women confront in the "real world." It is true that the creation or analysis of literary texts often have a very different methodology from that of work in the sciences. Yet this does not mean that literature does not address or affect the problems that women face in their daily lives. The representations of women's situations, their interactions with each other and with men, their actions and emotions, can shape in many significant ways the power relationships that feminist movements are challenging. Literature is a voice which both speaks experience and enacts theory, a voice which is crucial for new self-definitions.

I have raised questions concerning the usefulness of psychoanalytic and literary studies for feminism. Yet I must also ask how I, as a feminist (and a daughter) can critique the way in which I have occasionally used these two "parents." There is potential for several different kinds of problems resulting from my need and suspicion of these two. It is possible that my view of them will misrepresent what they are or could be, showing them as monolithic rather than complex and variable. It is also important not to try to compete with them or to place them in competition with each other. By respecting the differences among the three elements of this triad, it might be possible for them to share power between them in a way that has not always been possible in families.

Indeed, the number three seems most suited at this time for an exploration of power, indicating relational networks, rather than contests. Yet it is difficult to make use of the family paradigm while remaining critical of the traditions that go with it: the dominating father, the ineffectual mother, the selfish daughter. We can neither avoid these traditions completely nor allow them to perpetuate themselves by shaping all other structures according to themselves. This is both the difficulty and the value of feminism's occasional alliance with literature and psychoanalysis: showing the underlying structures of our culture is not enough, indeed, used incautiously this strategy may only seem to affirm these structures. It is necessary to recognize them, understand their purposes, and then begin to change or discard them. However, without knowing what they are or why they exist, why we have felt that we needed them for so long, change is very difficult if not impossible for we are actually fighting ourselves.

Challenging family structures that have existed for thousands of years is asking everyone to understand who they are in completely different ways. The two parental poles: father as Law, mother as prohibited desire, are the foundations of our culture. The child's imperative of assuming one or the other of these roles is the beginning of personality formation. The feminist revision of gender requires a re-examination of this imperative, and suggests that there are other possibilities.

An examination of the mother-daughter relation touches on many issues that are crucial to contemporary feminist thinking. It is clear that the maternal figure shapes in a number of ways the daughter's relation to her self. The mother, as well as giving birth to her daughter, engenders her: she is a primary influence on the way in which the daughter assumes her "femininity."[2] The mother both instructs her daughter and serves as a model for her and thus occasionally offers contradictory information on the role of Woman in our society. The daughter's recognition of her mother's power over her in contrast to the mother's relative powerlessness in her society is crucial to her acquisition of her role.

In this way the mother-daughter bond also shapes the daughter's relations with other women. It could be that the duplicity or disillusionment that can exist in the mother-daughter relation extends to these other relationships: if a woman has perceived her mother as powerless, she might not care to ally herself with others of inferior status. Yet it is also possible that her outrage at her mother's victimization by a misogynistic society would turn her toward other women in search of solidarity. It is also true that women, even though needing to establish their own individuality, can appreciate their mother's roles and thus come to celebrate a different women's domain. It is important to examine the variety of ways in which the mother-daughter relation influences a woman's view of herself and other women: women's participation in their own oppressions and in the oppression of other women will not be changed merely by modifying their relationships to men.

Even though in reading daughters' autobiographies I am emphasizing the effect of the mother on the daughter through the daughter's perspective, it must be remembered that this is one side of the story, not all of it. For to see the mother only in relation to the daughter is to continue a repression of the mother that has been part of the oppression of women. Therefore, I will try to maintain an awareness in my readings of these autobiographies of the two subjectivities that are in some way present in the daughter's self-representation: both the mother's and the daughter's. It is not easy, but it is possible, to read through the daughter's language to try to catch sight of that other, the mother.

Indeed, the view of subjectivity that is conveyed by an autobiography is a complex one: the reader is often aware of the distinctions between writer, narrator, and main character, and this awareness often affects the view of the other "characters" in this life. The reader of an autobiography knows that there is a difference between the writer's actual mother and the person that plays that role in the written text, and this knowledge helps to show the text as "autofiction," foregrounding the construction of the identity of both self and other.

The writing of the self is a process which differs for women and men for several reasons. Women are placed differently in relation to representation than men; lacking the same type of subject status as men, their ability to enunciate their subjectivity is problematized. Their relation to language can also be seen as more adversarial in that women have often been discouraged from expressing themselves, in speech but particularly in writing. The theorization of "feminine" identity that can be found in women's autobiographical writings is therefore duplicitous: both affirming and denying identity, both representing and questioning "femininity," autogynographies, as Domna Stanton calls them, have multiple, sometimes contradictory projects.[3] It is a multi-faceted view of the self that challenges monolithic definitions of "Woman," showing differences between women as well as within them.

Colette, Simone de Beauvoir, and Marguerite Duras are three writers who have had significant roles in the shaping of twentieth-century literature. Spanning the century, their work overlaps temporally but not stylistically: they exemplify some of the differences in women writers of our time. All three could be described as interested in women's "difference" yet in varied ways.[4] Colette's writings show a strong identification with and admiration for other women, showing them as vulnerable to men yet often ultimately stronger, more intelligent, more loving than their lovers or husbands. Simone de Beauvoir is famous for her denunciations of women's oppression, both in *Le deuxième sexe* and in her later writings. The women in her texts, fictional and non-fictional, are frequently more complex and interesting than her male characters, yet very differently from Colette, she does not represent a "feminine" continuum. Rather, she seems to suggest that women are socially constructed in such a way as to be more dependent on their relationships with others than men. Marguerite Duras has more explicitly shifted her views of women throughout her career. Although her earlier writings often present a woman's point of view, it was not until the 1970s that her writing was clearly based on the exploration of women's "difference." Her more recent work has moved away from this perspective. Yet overall her representations of women have frequently addressed their different relations to power, to desire, to subjectivity.

These writers are also significant for the representation of their own identities in their works. Each has written numerous autobiographies in which the situation or creation of a woman writer is presented in great detail. Each writer exposes certain aspects of her life to public regard yet for reasons that seem very different. Colette's famous statement on the difference between a self-portrait and a "model" seems designed to tease the reader, to captivate yet elude at the same time.[5] Simone de Beauvoir's autobiographical writings show almost the inverse of this strategy: she records her life as explicitly as possible, stating that she withholds information only if it would impinge on the privacy of another. It would seem that she wants to be known completely. Duras is perhaps in between these two: neither deliberately concealing (as far as the reader can tell) yet selectively revealing (if not occasionally misleading), her writing gives the impression of a continual search for knowledge of self which is not as dependent on the reader as the self-investigations of the other two writers.

The differences and similarities of these three writers give a view of twentieth-century women that does not answer all of our questions on the construction of "femininity" in our culture. Yet through comparing and contrasting some of their self-representations it is possible to begin to see the various ways in which it is constructed. The examinations of self and others, self and (m)other that can be found in these texts show women's agency in their lives, yet also seem to suggest that they are never completely independent. A woman's definition of her self has traditionally been perceived as more relational than a man's; while it is possible that each of these writers might agree with this, their work represents relatedness to others very differently. Indeed, these writers seem to see the structuring of the self by the environment in different ways. Each writer shows the family to be important in the formation of the individual, yet each has her own understanding of the process. Simone de Beauvoir emphasizes the ability of the individual to transcend her environment whereas both Colette and Duras give more importance to the force of familial and social influences (yet Colette sees this as generally positive and for Duras it is negative).

A reading of these autobiographies with psychoanalytic theory will show the interconnections between the psychological and the social, the mother-daughter relation as primal bond and as social function. I have organized my readings of these texts around different thematic elements for each writer. In a sense, I am reading certain motifs as symptoms which articulate what is often unsaid about the mother-daughter relationship. What I find in the interstices of the daughter's language is a mixture of feelings, memories, and images whose contradictions and ambivalences haunt and unsettle the more straightforward descriptions that are found in these writers' works. In this way my analysis of the mother-daughter relation comes to resemble a search for the mother who has so often been absent from our culture's representations, a mother who is neither the Good Mother nor the Bad Mother that our traditions have upheld, but a figure who challenges these categorizations.

The first chapter, on Colette, uses the motifs of mourning and jealousy to show an ambivalence which is not always obvious in Colette's descriptions of her beloved mother, Sido. In following these themes through *La maison de Claudine*, *La naissance du jour*, and *Sido*, I find a merging of commonly polarized concepts such as body and language, presence and absence. Luce Irigaray's work on the mother-daughter bond in *Ce sexe qui n'en est pas un*, *Et l'une ne bouge pas sans l'autre*, and *Le corps-à-corps avec la mère* helps to indicate the ways in which Colette's representations work toward a language of "femininity" based on circularity and equilibrium, fluidity and merging. Yet Irigaray's texts also work with the motifs of mourning and jealousy to reveal a need for individuation which coexists with Colette's desire to merge with her mother.

The chapter on Simone de Beauvoir shows a very different representation of the mother-daughter relation. The motifs of complicity and silence in *Mémoires d'une jeune fille rangée* and *Une mort très douce* elucidate Beauvoir's discomfort with the traditional "feminine" role that her mother played and tried to pass on to her. These symptoms express the tensions of a mother-daughter bond which the daughter feels that she must fight in order to save herself, yet which continues to elicit a strong emotional connection. Julia Kristeva's work on abjection and identification in *Pouvoirs de l'horreur* and *Histoires d'amour* describes the mingled repulsion and attraction which informs the infant's first awareness of the mother as other. This view of the pre-oedipal is helpful in analyzing Beauvoir's representations of her feelings for her mother: an uneasy identification with the mother divides this writer. The concept of "femininity" in these texts reveals ambivalence; it is often seen as a

situation of powerlessness yet the power of the bond between mother and daughter upsets gender hierarchy.

My chapter on Marguerite Duras shows how she develops the story of her relationship with her mother over the course of four texts: *Un barrage contre le Pacifique, L'Eden Cinéma, L'amant,* and *L'amant de la Chine du Nord.* Although the story that she tells is essentially the same in each text, the motifs of orality and specularity help to indicate important shifts in the view of self and other. Irigaray's discussion of mother and daughter mirroring elucidates subject-object oppositions; the different fears associated with orality addressed in Kristeva's work explicate the movements toward and away from the mother. In these texts the connections between the social and the psychological oppressions of women are clearly enunciated, showing "femininity" as a construct that is both imposed on women and that they assume, objectifying themselves to survive.

The conclusion focuses on the representation of "difference" in these writings: I ask in what ways this representation might show the commonalities between women without obscuring the differences between them. For finally my project is this: to explore what brings women together, how their identities can be both separate and joined, and in what ways their differences can strengthen the bonds between them.

Notes

[1] In *The Daughter's Seduction: Feminism and Psychoanalysis*, Jane Gallop envisions psychoanalysis as the father and feminism as the daughter. In "Entertaining the Ménage à Trois: Psychoanalysis, Feminism, and Literature," in *Feminism and Psychoanalysis*, edited by Richard Feldstein and Judith Roof, Jerry Aline Flieger adds literature as the mother.

[2] "Femininity" will be placed in quotes to recall that this concept is a social and theoretical construct whose meaning shifts according to the context in which it is used.

[3] See Domna Stanton's "Autogynography: Is the Subject Different?" in *The Female Autograph: Theory and Practice of Autobiography from the Tenth to the Twentieth Century.*

[4] "Difference" is in quotes to indicate a theorized difference between men and women.

[5] "Imaginez-vous, à me lire, que je fais mon portrait? Patience : c'est seulement mon modèle." This phrase is found both as epigraph on page 19 and (slightly modified) as part of the text on page 53 of *La naissance du jour*.

Chapter II

Mourning and Jealousy
in *La maison de Claudine*,
La naissance du jour, and *Sido*

Nous avons aussi à trouver, retrouver, inventer, découvrir, les paroles qui disent le rapport à la fois le plus archaïque et le plus actuel au corps de la mère, à notre corps, les phrases qui traduisent le lien entre son corps, le nôtre, celui de nos filles. Un langage qui ne se substitue pas au corps-à-corps, ainsi que le fait la langue paternelle mais qui l'accompagne, des paroles qui ne barrent pas le corporel mais qui parlent 'corporel'.

Le corps-à-corps avec la mère

The textual embodiment of the mother that Luce Irigaray is advocating in the passage chosen to begin this chapter is very pertinent to an analysis of Colette's writings on her mother. The notions of *parler-mère* and *parler-corps,* although modern, can be related to work that predates these formulations and might help us to understand differently the impact that Colette has had and continues to have. Irigaray's criticism of "la langue paternelle" suggests that women have always expressed themselves in a language which is not their own; they are foreigners speaking their native tongue. I would like to read Colette's work as a subversion of patriarchal language by the mother tongue, a writing which occasionally leaves gaps through which can be perceived the mother's body.

In recent years, certain feminist critics have recognized that Colette's works need to be read as much more than transparent autobiography.[1] Although it is very tempting to take the lyrical descriptions of Sido, her garden, and the surrounding countryside at face value and incorporate them into a celebration of the "materrenelle"—both Earth Mother and Mother Earth—this is a reductive treatment both of Colette's work and the subjects of her texts.[2] There is a constant interplay between "Colette" the narrator and "Gabrielle" the child who is presented in the three texts which will be examined here, creating a voice that is often posited as the child's point of view but which is filtered retrospectively through an adult consciousness.[3] Despite the temptation to participate in the child's dream of this perfect mother and childhood, it is important to remember the artifice involved in this seductive representation of Nature. In *La maison de Claudine, La naissance du jour,* and *Sido* the use of personal biography can often be read as addressing more general themes and mythemes of maternity, nature, creation and creativity.

This analysis of Colette's texts investigates what could be described as maternal metaphors in her work, reading these together with feminist psychoanalytic theory—primarily Luce Irigaray's writings on the mother-daughter relation—in order to trace the often uneasy balance between the function and the definition of the maternal in our culture. Irigaray's work addresses very specifically the unease located in our culture's mutilation of the maternal; I hope that her theories will open Colette's more "fictional" representations to new readings.

This analysis relies on an understanding of the pre-oedipal, a stage of human development that is often characterized as an idyllic union between mother and child. This union is ended by the intrusion of the father and the beginning of the Oedipus complex. Although Freud was the first to speak of the pre-oedipal, it was not until his later writings that he acknowledged both the importance of this stage for women, and his ignorance concerning its exact repercussions. Later theorists such as Melanie Klein developed more fully a theory of this stage. According to Klein, this is a time dominated by fear and rage; the infant feels helpless and tries to protect herself with phantasies of destruction carrried out on the body of the mother, the person who seems most powerful and most responsible for any lack or discomfort.

More recently, feminist psychoanalysts have theorized the pre-oedipal stage as a time of pleasure and innocence, finally spoiled by the father's intervention. Some feminist theoreticians posit this time as a blissful merging of mother and child in which the child is not yet aware of the distinction between self and other. The re-vision and valorization of this stage are crucial to feminist thinking in recovering a maternal figure who has been effaced throughout history. Not only does this important connection to the mother help us to understand better the construction and gendering of the ego, it also leads to a reformulation of female bonding in general.[4] Androcentric cultures amputate the personal history of men and women by denying the mother a place; the effects of this amputation on women surface in their writing on mothers and daughters. Colette's writing is an example of how this culturally obscured personal history can be uncovered and explored.

Luce Irigaray's attention to the pre-oedipal suggests both positive and negative aspects of this period, but she emphasizes women's need to recuperate this time and in this way create a relation to the mother. Beginning with *Speculum de l'autre femme,* Irigaray demonstrates through a re-reading of Western philosophers that the effacing of this relationship is the foundation of Western epistemology. In *Ce sexe qui n'en est pas un* she continues this critique and states that our culture is founded on matricide, rather than on the patricide hypothesized by Freud. Her short text *Et l'une ne bouge pas sans l'autre* explores the complexity of mother-daughter relations with an emphasis on the restrictions and dangers related to an oppressive interdependence. A later work, *Le corps-à-corps avec la mère,* discusses this relationship with a new recognition of women's connection to their mothers, noting that distancing between them can often be crippling. The two later texts would seem to advocate that women find a balance in their relationships with their mothers: in *Et l'une ne bouge pas sans l'autre,* too much closeness leads to paralysis, yet in *Le corps-à-corps avec la mère,* the lack of connection to the mother is linked to insanity.

The *parler-femme* which Irigaray both advocates and demonstrates in her texts is important to my understanding of Colette's work, making it possible to describe her writing as an inscription of "difference." However, the manner of this inscription is as difficult to articulate as "difference" itself. Irigaray's texts give some indications:

> Ce 'style' ne privilégie pas le regard mais rend toute figure à sa naissance, aussi *tactile*. Elle s'y re-touche sans jamais y constituer, s'y constituer en quelque unité. La *simultanéité* serait son 'propre'. Un propre qui ne s'arrête jamais dans la possible identité à soi d'aucune forme. Toujours *fluide,* sans oublier les caractères difficilement idéalisables de ceux-ci : ces frottements entre deux infiniment voisins qui font dynamique. Son 'style' résiste à, et fait exploser, toute forme, figure, idée, concept, solidement établis. (*Ce sexe* 76)

This language which speaks woman, speaks body, speaks the relation to the mother's body is itself elusive, yet there is something of this to be found in Colette's work. It is as though Irigaray is directing us to "speak body," whereas Colette shows us what happens when we let the body speak. The problem is to speak our relation to something that has been excised from our history, both personal and societal. In this sense our language becomes perhaps a dis-covery of this body and the act of speaking becomes merged with the act of excavation. Women's search for the mother tongue becomes a search for her body as well.

Hélène Cixous, whose work on *écriture féminine* is close to Irigaray's conception of a *parler-femme*, describes woman writing in this way:

> Elle ne retient pas, d'où les effets de ré-apparition permanente que provoque le ne-pas-retenir. C'est comme une sorte de mémoire ouverte qui laisse passer sans cesse. ("Le sexe ou la tête" 15)

This description evokes several important aspects of the writings of Colette. Particularly in the writings which are more concerned with her mother, different periods are merged in a synchronic collapsing of time rather than a diachronic development. This "mémoire ouverte" produces a language which flows back and forth from a narrative present to different moments of childhood, adolescence, or young womanhood. The "ré-apparition permanente" or oscillation in this work is both a temporal play and a balancing between the realm of language and that which cannot be said.

Irigaray's theorization of a pre-platonic "poiétique" speech could also be useful in a discussion of Colette's style: it is "une parole qui n'est pas l'énoncé de la vérité mais une parole qui fait vérité, qui agit, mais pas du tout dans une hiérarchie fiction/théorie" (*Le corps-à-corps* 45). This examination of the relation of speech to truth, of fiction to theory is a deconstructive move in that Irigaray does not simply elevate one term to increased importance while correspondingly lowering the other; rather, it becomes more difficult to accept the arbitrary polarizations upon which hierarchy is based. Irigaray's writings refuse binary polarizations, instead they attempt to transform or merge what could be seen as "positive" and "negative" in the mother-daughter relation. Her use of language to reveal the "feminine" which the language itself has always obscured, involves what could be described as a constant flickering or slippage between polarized concepts: good/bad, presence/absence, meaning/non-meaning, all are inverted and emptied of their usual value. This is a writing which embodies oscillation, in this way escaping from teleological *logos*.

Following Irigaray's lead we must question such labels for Colette's work as "womanly," "earthy," or "non-intellectual." It is necessary to re-examine these terms outside of the polarizations: womanly/manly, earthy/abstract, non-intellectual/intellectual in order to resituate this work in a "feminine" genealogy.[5] Colette's imbrication of the themes of creation and memory, perhaps creation of memory, in her representation of her mother and her childhood seems to approach the "parole poiétique" which Irigaray describes. Her writing evades common hierarchies and challenges the notion of truth as something which is simply apprehended through the medium of language.

It is also important to note what might seem to be oppositions in the work of these two writers: while Irigaray addresses the suppression and repression of the Mother in our society, Colette's mother is predominant. Irigaray's Mother is a faceless, archaic victim; Colette's mother is often shown to be the one upon whom others are dependent. Irigaray's Mother seems to be fragmented and amputated; Colette's mother is portrayed as the epitome of plenitude. Simply, it is possible to contrast Irigaray's missing Mother to Colette's Eternal mother. However, these efforts to expose what has been hidden or to display what has been considered private could be described as sharing similar goals: a view of what has been invisible, a voice for what has been unspeakable.

Yet, in the case of each of these writers, there is more to be said, more to be seen. Colette's portrayal of Sido both resists and is complicitous with the patriarchal hegemony. Her creation of her mother according to her own needs and desires is still somewhat of a reification, a transformation of Sido to "Sido." The distinction between the needs of "Gabrielle" and "Colette" is not always clear: the writer's representation of her mother would seem to oscillate between "Gabrielle's" need for a mother who is completely available to her, and "Colette's" recognition that Sido has her own needs. In her writing Colette makes visible a merged character "Gabrielle"/"Colette" who wants to reduce her mother to the object of her daughter's needs yet recognizes that this limits and oppresses her.

The character of "Sido" is not as uncomplicated as some readings of Colette's work have assumed; although portrayed as weighted down by husband and children, she is still not presented as dominated by them. Colette frequently insists on her mother's freedom—freedom from tradition, from social constraints, from the commonplace—yet this is made ambivalent by the fact that the writer must take two stances simultaneously, that of the child who needs to feel the mother's unconditional presence and love, and that of the adult writer who seems sometimes to be urging freedom and escape retroactively as she writes. Similarly, in her treatment of Sido as an instrument of the patriarchy who must form her daughters into suitable women, the reader is given two views of this function: through the child "Gabrielle's" eyes we see a dutiful wife and mother combing her daughters' long hair and reassuring them about childbirth. However, narrative distance shows a woman who is unhappy when it is time for her daughters to marry and who finds the institutions of love and marriage ignoble and untrustworthy. Colette splits her narrative representation into different points of view and thus portrays a woman divided against herself, a complex view that addresses the situation of women as mothers and daughters in her society.

While Colette's descriptions seem to move from the particular (her mother) to the general (women's relationships with women in our society), Irigaray's writing refuses these categories. Her theorization of the Mother is deliberately blurred, incomplete, and fluid, trying to avoid universalizing or essentializing this figure. Her work is an attempt to represent the unrepresentable; it is a discourse of enigma, an enunciation made up of holes and fragments. In showing the Mother's absence from Western culture she shows an abyss. The revelation of the Mother's murder undermines the referentiality of language in its revelation of what has never been (thought).

In this sense Irigaray's project is always necessarily contradictory: the revelation/representation of something that has never been and cannot be revealed or represented becomes a spiral of language which tries to open into new ways of perceiving and thinking. This use of language intersects with the work of other writers, explicating the underlying contradictions that disrupt their work as well. Colette's disjunctive vision elucidates the contradictions of trying to place her mother as Sido, the subject of her own life, and "Sido," representing the maternal function/fiction. Both of these writers are addressing what cannot be said about the M/m/other due to the repression and suppression imposed on her by our culture.

At the end of *La naissance du jour*, Colette describes her mother's last letter as almost hieroglyphic in its abandonment of an old worn-out language.

> Deux feuillets crayonnés ne portent plus que des signes qui semblent joyeux, des flèches partant d'un mot esquissé, de petits rayons, deux 'oui, oui' et un 'elle a dansé' très net. Elle a écrit aussi, plus bas, 'mon amour' — elle m'appelait ainsi quand nos séparations se faisaient longues.... (166–7)

This mingling of signs and affirmations, movement and emotion incorporates the mother's discorporation. As Sido prepares to leave her life, her writing becomes a countryside where are hidden "un visage dans les feuilles, un bras entre deux branches, un torse sous des noeuds de rochers..." (167). Language and body fragment and rejoin in new ways; Colette is creating the maternal body as text. In this layering of transformations we find the *parler-femme*, *parler-corps*, and *parler-mère* of Irigaray. Through this disintegration of the mother's body and language at the same time the reader comes to glimpse the face of a different figure who speaks a different language. This enigmatic figure is left as open and unfinished as the final sentence of the text: "[L]e voici halliers, embruns, météores, livre sans bornes ouvert, grappe, navire, oasis..." (167). This final paragraph's description of dawn as "le moment qui enfante le jour" continues the maternal imagery yet it is perhaps the ellipsis (that which signifies absence) that most clearly recalls both Colette's mother Sido and Irigaray's Mother still waiting to speak.

Mourning

> [J]e sentis remuer au fond de moi celle qui maintenant m'habite, plus légère à mon coeur que je ne fus jadis à son flanc....
>
> *La naissance du jour*

Of the many motifs which structure Colette's writings and give them their coherent unity, I have chosen to focus on two that could be read as symptomatic of Colette's challenge to the reification of the maternal in *La maison de Claudine, La naissance du jour,* and *Sido*. Mourning is the first of these motifs: as all three texts were written after the death of Colette's mother, the confrontation of this loss is articulated in each text, most obviously in *La naissance du jour* in which the mother's presence or absence is central to the text. The second motif that will be examined is that of jealousy in the various forms in which it appears in this family: the competition between children and father for Sido's attention, Sido's possessiveness concerning her children, a rivalry between mother and daughter which is mentioned but not elaborated upon.

These two reactions of "Colette"/"Gabrielle" to her mother—mourning her and being jealous of/about her—are areas in which a tension can be seen in the individuation of mother and daughter. Both mourning and jealousy can be indicative of a troubling of identity in that each of these emotions is based on the actual or anticipated loss of another. The confrontation of a need for the other which must remain unsatisfied destabilizes the ego, challenging any illusion of an autonomous self. In "Mourning and Melancholia" Freud discusses a possible result of this: "The loss of a love-object is an excellent opportunity for the ambivalence in love-relationships to make itself effective and come into the open" (250–51). It is possible that this ambivalence problematizes Colette's represented relationship to her mother and to her self. Colette's portrayal of her reactions to her mother's absence—real (through death) or imagined (through turning away to another)—helps to invert more common readings of these texts: although known as texts of maternal plenitude and presence, they incorporate as well the problem of maternal absence. In the same way that Colette moves back and forth temporally to recreate this time, there is also a back and forth movement between mother and daughter: the two are sometimes almost merged, other times further apart. An examination of these motifs will help to show this instability.

Colette's first text on her mother, *La maison de Claudine,* was published in 1922, ten years after her mother's death. The other two texts in which her mother is the central figure were written within the decade: *La naissance du jour* was published in 1928, *Sido* in 1929–30. For each of these three texts, I will try to show how Colette's use of the theme of mourning opens up an exploration of self-identity. I believe that it will be useful to contrast Colette's descriptions of her mother and to note how these descriptions inflect the view of the writer that is presented to the reader. In the confrontation of loss the polarization of presence/absence is challenged: as we will see in *La naissance du jour,* Sido is represented as almost more present to her daughter after her death. The different kind of presence which is "Sido's" in *La naissance du jour* destabilizes both presence/absence and life/death oppositions by pluralizing the maternal identity; the daughter's creation of the mother speaks a lack of differentiation in this mother-daughter relation.

For Irigaray the mother-daughter relation seems necessarily to be founded on a series of losses: loss of the mother means loss of the self or perhaps a recognition that the self has always been absent.

> A chacune, sa représentation fait défaut. Son visage, l'animation de son corps manque. Et l'une porte le deuil de l'autre. (*Et l'une ne bouge pas sans l'autre* 20)

In this description of the mother-daughter relationship it would seem that as each is not represented to herself, she is not present, to herself or to the other. Here mourning signifies an absence of identity which engulfs the mother-daughter dyad. It is a *mise en abîme* of mirrors reflecting emptiness. While this is a powerful description of the dangers of merged identities, the emphasis on representation suggests a possible way out of the *abîme*.

> Il nous faudra en quelque sorte faire le deuil d'une toute-puissance maternelle (le dernier refuge) et établir avec nos

> mères un rapport de réciprocité de femme à femme.... (*Le corps-à-corps* 86)

In this later work Irigaray's position on the mother-daughter bond has shifted: mourning clearly helps to heal rather than merely reflecting loss and negation. Irigaray believes that it is necessary to represent our loss (*porter le deuil*) in order to survive it. It seems that somewhere in between the "toute-puissance maternelle" or phallic mother, and the lack or non-representation which is the other extreme of the maternal construct in our culture, women must imagine another possibility. Colette's representations of the loss of the mother could be described as approaching this project.

In the story called "Le rire" in *La maison de Claudine,* there is an account of Sido's behavior after the funeral of her husband. First she proclaims her impatience with the custom of wearing mourning:

> J'ai horreur de ce noir! D'abord c'est triste. Pourquoi veux-tu que j'offre, à ceux que je rencontre, un spectacle triste et déplaisant? Quel rapport y a-t-il entre ce cachemire et ce crêpe et mes propres sentiments? Que je te voie jamais porter mon deuil! Tu sais très bien que je n'aime pour toi que le rose, et certains bleus... (114)

Much of this passage is concerned with the representation of loss. Sido's distinctions between feeling and ritual, symbol and action could be said to enunciate the writer's own concerns with living with loss while at the same time positing the (lost) mother as authority. In other words, Colette uses "Sido," the figure of the mother, to question socially imposed representations which falsify loss rather than confronting it. "Sido's" assumption of continued presence after death, "Que je te voie jamais porter mon deuil!" also challenges established ontology: death is reduced to a representation of absence.

The passage which immediately follows the one just quoted continues with the mother's challenge to convention and to common oppositions:

> Et elle riait, ma mère en deuil, elle riait de son rire aigu de jeune fille, et frappait dans ses mains devant le petit chat...Le souvenir fulgurant tarit cette cascade brillante, sécha dans les yeux de ma mère les larmes du rire. Pourtant, elle ne s'excusa pas d'avoir ri, ni ce jour-là, ni ceux qui suivirent, car elle nous fit cette grâce, ayant perdu celui qu'elle aimait d'amour, de demeurer parmi nous toute pareille à elle-même, acceptant sa douleur ainsi qu'elle eût accepté l'avènement d'une saison lugubre et longue, mais recevant de toutes parts la bénédiction passagère de la joie, — elle vécut balayée d'ombre et de lumière, courbée sous des tourmentes, résignée, changeante et généreuse, parée d'enfants, de fleurs et d'animaux comme un domaine nourricier. (115)

The series of comparisons, contrasts, and oppositions that are shown to be not really opposed in this passage expresses on another level what is expressed by the juxtaposition of the title and subject of this story: laughter and mourning are not contradictory or mutually exclusive, they can coexist as can loss and joy, light and dark, change and resignation. This juxtaposition is emphasized by the fact that in this scene of sorrow it is tears of laughter that are dried. There are thus two movements taking place in these passages: a distinction is being made between different representations of loss, yet there is a merging of categories that are generally perceived as polarized. Colette's representation of the loss of the mother is in this text more focused on the mother's experience of loss. In this writing "Sido" represents Colette's model for herself.[6] As in other stories in *La maison de Claudine,* Colette's portrayal of "Sido" is a seamless return to the mother, both inscribing her life and showing the desire to pattern her own life on this model.[7]

In a story called "Ma mère et les livres," Sido makes a promise to her daughter to return as a ghost after her death:

> Ce doit être ravissant, un fantôme. Je voudrais bien en voir un, je t'appellerais. Malheureusement ils n'existent pas. Si je pouvais me faire fantôme après ma vie, je n'y manquerais pas,

> pour ton plaisir et pour le mien. (*La maison de Claudine* 34)

This promise is, in a sense, realized in *La naissance du jour*. Colette's story of the renunciation of sexual love is interwoven with a dialogue with her mother, addressed as "ma chère revenante" or described as a "fantôme maternel." The continual evocation of her presence along with the inclusion of letters supposedly written by Sido make it seem that the book was written by the two women. "D'elle, de moi, qui donc est le meilleur écrivain? N'éclate-t-il pas que c'est elle?" (165). In fact, the notion of authorship is problematized in this text as it is made up of Colette's narration and selected letters of Sido which she quotes after having altered or invented them.[8]

This manner of incorporating her mother into the text has many effects, challenging established conventions of identity as well as the opposition of presence/absence. By taking on her mother's voice Colette chooses to merge the two identities. This merging begins with a short prologue based on a letter of Sido's (rewritten) which is followed by a classically structured litany of statements beginning "Je suis la fille de..." affirming what has become an increasingly important maternal legacy. This relationship is confirmed on another level by an increasing physical similarity: "[M]aintenant que je me défais peu à peu et que dans le miroir peu à peu je lui ressemble..." (20). The use of the verb "se défaire" meaning to come undone is worth noting here: it would seem that "Colette" is fragmenting, that age brings not only a different relationship to the body but also to the psyche. "Colette's" "coming undone" allows her to incorporate her mother's presence. The introductory passage ends with yet another comparison, imagining that the mother's ghost would also see the similarities in their lives despite seeming differences:

> 'Ecarte-toi, laisse que je voie, me dirait ma très chère revenante...Ah! n'est-ce pas mon cactus rose qui me survit, et que tu embrasses? Qu'il a singulièrement grandi et changé...Mais en interrogeant ton visage, ma fille, je le

reconnais.'(21)

In this way the text begins with a series of comparisons which reflect the diminishing of separation between mother and daughter.

Following this opening attention to resemblances to the maternal figure, Colette focuses on language in order to foreground differences:

> Quand je tâche d'inventer ce qu'elle m'eût dit, il y a toujours un point de son discours où je suis défaillante. Il me manque les mots, surtout l'argument essentiel, le blâme, l'indulgence imprévus, pareillement séduisants, et qui tombaient d'elle, légers, lents à toucher mon limon et à s'y enliser doucement, lents à resurgir. Ils resurgissent maintenant de moi, et quelquefois on les trouve beaux. Mais je sais bien que, reconnaissables, ils sont déformés selon mon code personnel. (45–6)

Here is the writer as transmitter of the mother's words, trying to reproduce what has formed her yet admitting her deformation of this heritage. Whereas in the prologue there was a movement of merging personalities despite differences, here we find an effort to reproduce the mother's voice which is hindered by differences. The search for the mother tongue turns this text inside out. The mother's writing is a pretext for the daughter's creation which is, in a way, the reproduction of the mother. The focus on the mother tongue confuses the notion of the narrator once again: despite the fact that Colette acknowledges the differences between the two women, there is a merging of voices. "Je te remets le soin, ma compagne subtile, de louer un [homme] que tu n'as pas connu" (155). The lives and reactions of the two women thus appear to be somewhat interchangeable.

The internalized maternal presence resembles Irigaray's description of a new type of bonding possible between women:

> Déjà, je te transporte avec moi partout. Non comme un

enfant, un fardeau, un poids. Même aimé, même précieux. Tu n'es pas *en moi*. Je ne te contiens ni ne te retiens : dans mon ventre, mes bras, ma tête. Ni ma mémoire, mon esprit, mon langage. Tu es là, telle la vie de ma peau. (*Ce sexe* 215)

Although the essay "Quand nos lèvres se parlent," from which this quotation is taken, is addressed to a woman who is not the mother, "[P]ardon ma mère, je vous préfère une femme" (*Ce sexe* 208), its blurring of the boundaries between inside/outside, body/mind, womb/memory are very pertinent to the symbiosis which Colette creates with her mother in *La naissance du jour*. Each writer speaks of her relationship as coexistence. In each we see a collapsing of categories that are not polarized yet do not completely merge, leaving room for difference without opposition.

Colette's invocation/evocation of her mother's presence is not a denial of death but a refusal to separate death from life. "D'autres jours, je me vois...forcée de concéder une large hospitalité à ceux qui m'ayant cédé leur place sur la terre, ne se sont qu'en apparence immergés dans la mort" (156). In this text the dead are almost more present than the living. The ghost of the mother challenges the opposition of the terms life/death as well as those of presence/absence and self/other.

There are significant differences between the representation of "Sido" in *La maison de Claudine* and in *La naissance du jour*. Whereas Colette's recollection of her mother in the first text was a smoothly coherent and admiring description, the second text has more breaks and hesitations in the portrayal of the mother-daughter relation. They are similar but different, there is a distance as well as a merging. The final reference to Sido in *La naissance du jour* is the description of the mother's final letter: "[M]a mère en l'écrivant voulut sans doute m'assurer qu'elle avait déjà quitté l'obligation d'employer notre langage" (166). Although Colette does not translate this letter for the reader as she has tried to transmit her mother's language at other moments, it is clear that she understands it: "[J]'y lis un de ces paysages hantés où par jeu l'on cacha un visage dans les feuilles, un bras entre deux branches, un torse sous des noeuds de rochers..." (167). Thus the end of this text which speaks about the mother, and to the mother, and with the mother, leaves the reader with the image of a *different* mother-daughter language than the one in which this text was written, a language which is a haunted landscape. The "paysage hanté" denounces any presence/absence opposition: in a sense this entire text is haunted by Sido who is there but invented, gone but saturating her daughter's writing. Throughout these two texts the metonymic chain of references to ghosts, spirits, and hauntings recalls the Lacanian definition of desire as an endless movement referring back to the loss of the mother. In *La naissance du jour* the loss of the mother is simultaneously refused and accepted; by internalizing her mother Colette succeeds in both losing and holding her.

The last of Colette's texts on her mother is *Sido,* written eighteen years after her death. The focus here is not on the death of Colette's mother or on her presence/absence to her daughter, but rather on a representation more fragmented, less serene than in either of the two preceding texts. The most significant contrast to *La naissance du jour* is precisely the maternal absence. When Colette visits a clairvoyant and asks if her mother can be seen, the response is that she is not there and is probably with Colette's brother. That is all that is said on the subject. This is an interesting contrast to the presence of the "fantôme" of *La naissance du jour.* The surprising absence seems to be related to a different type of representation of the mother. More than the other two texts which have been analyzed here, *Sido* shows a woman who is sometimes constrained by family and obligations to deny herself, or perhaps to acknowledge only one half of herself. In *Sido,* Colette sees her mother more as a woman than as simply Gabrielle's mother; there is a "réciprocité de femme à femme" that comes perhaps from having completed her mourning. Once Colette can step outside of the child's need for the all-giving mother, she can portray Sido with her own thoughts, needs, and desires.

Dans ses yeux passa une sorte de frénésie riante, un universel mépris, un dédain dansant qui me foulait avec tout le

> reste, allégrement...Ce ne fut qu'un moment, — non pas un moment unique. Maintenant que je la connais mieux, j'interprète ces éclairs de son visage. Il me semble qu'un besoin d'échapper à tout et à tous, un bond vers le haut, vers une loi écrite par elle seule, pour elle seule, les allumait. Si je me trompe, laissez-moi errer. (23)

There are several important differences between the tone of this passage and that of the earlier texts. There is no longer the same privileging of the mother-daughter relation that was so fundamental in *La maison de Claudine* and *La naissance du jour*. Sido leaves everyone behind including her daughter. Colette's position as the writer who recounts, invents, tries to transmit her mother's words, has also changed: here she interprets while admitting the possible error of her interpretation. In this text "Sido" is a woman divided; this becomes even more clear in the paragraph that immediately follows the one just cited:

> Sous le cerisier, elle retomba encore une fois parmi nous, lestée de soucis, d'amour, d'enfants et de mari suspendus, elle redevint bonne, ronde, humble devant l'ordinaire de sa vie.... (23)

Sido returns to her role, putting an end to the moment of freedom in which she identified with a bird's arrogance and beauty.[9]

Returning to the puzzling absence noted when Colette visits the clairvoyant, the answer could be that in this text Colette is giving her mother the freedom that previously she could scarcely acknowledge as a possible need. Mourning is over, separation is accomplished, the visit to the clairvoyant is not inspired by sorrow or loss but, she informs the reader, only her usual curiosity. The absence of the mother is accepted as perfectly normal in a way that it could not be in the two earlier texts. It is interesting that the first of these begins with a story titled "Où sont les enfants?" in which the loving "mère-chienne" looks for her independent children. *La naissance du jour* is based on the certainty that she is there, still looking after her children. In *Sido* she has been released, perhaps, from "mother" to Sido—that is why there is no mourning for her in this text, but an acknowledgement of her life as it must have been: sometimes difficult, divided, both fulfilling and limiting.

In *Le corps-à-corps avec la mère* Irigaray discusses problems that result from boundary confusion between mother and daughter.

> Je connais des femmes qui, après la mort de leur mère, se tapent des cauchemars...les revenants...les fantômes qui parlent...du fait qu'il n'y a pas d'identité bien tranchée entre ces deux femmes. La mère meurt, mais s'il n'y a pas vraiment une identité pour les deux, dans la mort de cette mère il y a ces questions : 'Est-ce que je ne suis pas morte aussi? Est-ce que ce n'est pas moi qui l'ai tuée? Est-ce que je n'avais pas besoin qu'elle meure pour exister?' (62–3)

Here we see the dangers of merged identities: because the mother has not been allowed into life, her death implicates the life of her daughter. Equally, as the daughter has not been able to give her mother the life that she has been denied, she is complicitous in her death. Irigaray suggests that it would be better to mourn our mothers and the relationship that we never had with them and then we would be able to create a different relation to this person who, whether present in our lives or not, will always be central in our existence. One could almost reverse the myth of Demeter and Persephone to understand this idea: in the myth it is the mother whose mourning for her kidnapped daughter finally succeeds in reuniting mother and daughter who are allowed to spend half of the year together. There is an echo of this theme in Irigaray's suggestion: if daughters can learn to mourn their mothers (in some way taken from them), they can at least partially heal this loss.

Mourning is an important structuring concept for each of these two writers in part due to its circularity: there is a validation of death in life and life in death, making use of one to return to or affirm the other. The rejection of linearity that can be found in the writings of both Irigaray and Colette is an important appeal simultaneously to past and future: to a pre-patriarchal tradition and to the potential for changing a "teleologic" that cannot speak the "feminine." Mourning the mother can be seen equally as a return to an earlier idyllic time and as a movement toward a new "feminine" unity in which we could be both separate from and linked to our mothers.

Mourning in the three texts of Colette takes different forms: the first represented the mother as model, confronting the contradictions involved with loss. In the second the writer invokes her absent yet even more present mother in order to learn to face loss of various kinds. In the third, both of the areas of ambiguity that were noted —identity and presence/absence—are apparently resolved. The mother is gone, the identities of mother and daughter are presented as more separate. Colette's need to evoke, invent, transform and finally liberate "Sido" is represented as a process which perhaps begins with her mother's death. The issues of merging and distance, absence and presence, and difference without opposition are put into play in an exploration of creation and identity, and creation *of* identity, showing that even this famous and loving bond is not as immutable as it might seem.

Jealousy

> L'onde de fureur qui monte en moi et me gouverne comme un plaisir des sens...la jalousie qui me rendit, autrefois, si incommode...
>
> *La naissance du jour*

In addition to noting the suppression of the mother, contemporary feminist theoreticians have suggested that perhaps the most severe prohibitions have been applied to the mother's sexual desire and pleasure. When examining the interplay of jealousy at the heart of "the family romance," one must first consider the importance and force of the repression of maternal *jouissance*.

> Le désir d'elle, son désir à elle, voilà ce que doit venir interdire la loi du père — de tous les pères. (*Le corps-à-corps* 15)

Irigaray points out in the passage from which this excerpt is quoted that it is actually two types of "mother desire" that have been suppressed, repressed, and denied: the mother's desire and desire for the mother. This dual prohibition is the basis of many of the tensions in the family. Not only is the mother not allowed to feel desire, but the child's desire for the mother must be repressed; for a male child, this problem is resolved by his fear of castration, for a female child, already "castrated," it is different.

> [L]es femmes, étant donné que le premier corps auquel elles ont à faire, le premier amour auquel elles ont à faire étant un amour maternel, étant un corps de femme, les femmes sont toujours — à moins de renoncer à leur désir — dans un certain rapport archaïque et primaire à ce qu'on appelle homo-sexualité. (*Le corps-à-corps* 30)

This privileged correspondance between the mother's and daughter's bodies could involve special difficulties in a daughter's acceptance of the father. Thus denial of maternal *jouissance* can have two sources: the patriarchal need to contain and control this subversive force, and the child's need to deny that the mother could have any desire outside the mother-child dyad.[10] Irigaray addresses the contradiction that results from this deformation of the mother: "[E]lle renonce au plaisir qui lui vient de la *non-suture de ses lèvres* : mère sans doute mais vierge..." (*Ce sexe* 29). Although Irigaray is speaking here of male suppression of female sexuality, the concept of "mère-vierge" might be important for both husband and daughter. While relatively little has been said about daughters' possessiveness concerning their mothers (which is in itself another type of denial of female sexuality), it would be an understandable reaction. Colette's representation of her family gives jealousy a central role but it is not always predictable or stable: mother and daughter are occasionally possessive of each other, but it is also admitted that they can be rivals.

While Irigaray does not address the concept of jealousy as explicitly as she addresses that of mourning, it is not difficult to find in her work an enunciation of the problems of the entangled relation that exists between mother and daughter.

> Tu me gardes, tu me regardes. Tu désires toujours que je sois sous tes yeux pour me protéger. (*Et l'une ne bouge pas* 8)

Although in this short text it is for the most part the mother's jealous possessiveness toward the daughter which is represented, Irigaray's focus on the mirroring and merging that are always present in the mother-daughter relationship enunciates the ambivalence that is necessarily an aspect of a more fragile ego autonomy. In Irigaray's writings both mother and daughter seem to alternate in movements of attraction and repulsion which continually shift and replace each other. There are simultaneous needs for closeness and for distance which maintain the two women in a *corps-à-corps* (embrace/clinch) that cannot end without mutual destruction.

In "Ma mère et la maladie" in *La maison de Claudine,* one of Sido's statements seems an abrupt denial of the mother-daughter bond more consistently presented in these texts, with an apparent priority given to her relationship with her son: "Oui, oui, tu m'aimes, mais tu es une fille, une bête femelle, ma pareille et ma rivale. Lui, j'ai toujours été sans rivale dans son coeur" (118). Mentions of the special attachment between mothers and their eldest sons are rare in these three texts, and this is the only overt mention of rivalry between Colette and Sido. Thus this statement's impact: in much of Colette's work there is an assumption that similarity creates cohesion, but here it is the opposite. An interesting asymmetry can also be seen in Sido's comment: she does not say, "My son is not my rival," but, "I have no rivals for my son." The mother-daughter and mother-son relations are not exactly in opposition, they are different. The story finishes with the complicity of the two women preparing for a man's visit, as close as ever, yet for a moment, with Sido's casual remark, the reader has the impression of something that is usually hidden surging forth.

This impression is given more weight by a story called "La Toutouque" earlier in the text about a very gentle dog whose rivalry with another female dog for the affections of a male turns her into an unrecognizable and savage creature. Colette describes her transformation: "Elle essaya son sourire de bonne nourrice, mais elle haletait, et le blanc de ses yeux, strié de filets sanguins, semblait saigner..." (90). The description of the dog as "bonne nourrice" is repeated several times in the story and serves to remind the reader that both of these stories, "Ma mère et la maladie" and "La Toutouque," are narrated from a daughter's point of view. In "Ma mère et la maladie," although a divorced woman, "Colette's" role is that of a daughter; in "La Toutouque" it is a ten-year-old's point of view. Thus what we find in each case is a daughter's representation of the unpredictability of the maternal figure; the schizophrenia of love, equally warm tenderness and savage possessiveness, is shown to exist in mothers despite what their children might like to believe. Colette does not or cannot address any disappointment concerning Sido, but it could be deflected onto her reaction to the beloved dog:

— Oh! Toutouque...Toutouque...
Je ne trouvais pas d'autres paroles, et ne savais comment me plaindre, m'effrayer et m'étonner qu'une force malfaisante, dont le nom même échappait à mes dix ans, pût changer en brute féroce la plus douce des créatures... (90)

The name that this ten-year-old could not enunciate is that of desire, that emotion forbidden to the maternal realm. The parallels between "La Toutouque" and "Ma mère et la maladie" are clear: as strong as the mother-daughter bonds might be, they will not always withstand the desire for the male. Indeed, one might wonder what "illness" is referred to in the title of "Ma mère et la maladie."

Another short story about animals in *La maison de Claudine* speaks precisely of the mother-son bond. In "Les deux chattes" Colette recounts the adoption/seduction of Kamaralzaman, a young male cat, by a mother cat, Noire du Voisin, whose kittens have been drowned. The manner in which the bereaved mother lures the kitten from his own mother, Moune, is phrased as an infidelity.

> [Moune] ne se trompait pas : l'impudente Noire et Kamaralzaman, l'un tétant l'autre, mêlés, heureux, gisaient sur la première marche, dans l'ombre, au bas de l'escalier où se précipita Moune — et où je la reçus dans mes bras, molle, privée de sentiment, évanouie comme une femme... (139)

This passage could very easily be read as a story of a woman discovering her lover with another woman: the illicit couple intertwined and flaunting their happiness, the betrayed woman suffering so much from the sight of their pleasure that she faints. Maternal love and sexual passion are not always distinct from each other in these stories. The title of this last story maintains the confusion as "chatte" is also a slang term for the female genitals, blurring both the separation between maternity and sexuality, and between animal and human. The blending of human and animal in this text helps to redefine maternal desire and maternal instinct as something almost unrecognizable.

In *La naissance du jour*, Colette refers again to a mother's possessiveness concerning the eldest son:

> Entre la mère encore jeune et une mûre maîtresse, c'est la rivalité du don qui empoisonne deux coeurs féminins et crée une haine glapissante, une guerre de renardes où la clameur maternelle n'est ni la moins sauvage, ni la moins indiscrète. (51)

Again there are at least two types of assimilation in this passage: mother love is indistinguishable from sexual jealousy and possessiveness, and it can be so savage as to transform the mother into an enraged vixen. The representation of maternal passion is linked in these texts to fury; the mother's desire for sons and lovers (perhaps the two together) becomes a force that can overwhelm all else.

In this text Colette also describes her mother's metamorphosis:

> Me voici contrainte, pour la renouer à moi, de rechercher le temps où ma mère rêvait dramatiquement au long de l'adolescence de son fils aîné, le très beau, le séducteur. En ce temps-là, je la devinai sauvage, pleine de fausse gaîté et de malédictions, ordinaire, enlaidie, aux aguets...Ah! que je la revoie ainsi diminuée, la joue colorée d'un rouge qui lui venait de la jalousie et de la fureur! (43)

As in Sido's comment on rivalry in "Ma mère et la maladie," this description is a surprising departure from Colette's usual portrayal of her mother. It seems that there is expressed in this text an almost reluctant desire to diminish the moral superiority that the writer herself has conferred: "Toi-même, ma très chère, toi que je voulais pure de mes crimes ordinaires, voilà que je trouve..." (51). In each of these texts, it is males who cause problems between females. Both the mother in general and Colette's mother in particular are represented as diminished by a possessive passion that transforms "en brute féroce la plus douce des créatures." This terrifying metamorphosis is a flaw in Sido, and thus in all mothers, which Colette does not frequently address.

When talking about her own jealousy Colette describes it as inherited from her father:

> L'onde de fureur qui monte en moi et me gouverne comme un plaisir des sens : voilà mon père, sa blanche main italienne tendue vers les lames, refermée sur le poignard à ressort qui ne le quittait pas. Mon père encore, la jalousie qui me rendit, autrefois, si incommode... (156–7)

This is almost the only mention of Colette's father in this entire text devoted to the renunciation of sexual love of men, and a return to the simplicity of childhood. It is he, of course, who has the mother in a way that her children cannot have her—as a sexual partner.

Therefore it is of him that Colette might be jealous. Yet this possibility is not acknowledged overtly. It could be, however, that Colette's reaction to her jealousy of the attachment between her parents is to take her mother from her father after their deaths. In other words, Colette's re-creation of "Sido" (including her adoption of this name for her mother that only her father used) could be seen as a claim of her mother's love and attention that would cover over any deficiencies that she might have felt. The father, so often missing from these stories of childhood, or given secondary importance, is being deliberately excluded to satisfy a child's desire to possess the mother exclusively. While "Sido's" possessiveness is depicted rarely in these texts, Colette's is even less acknowledged. Moreover, even when admitting to it, she distances herself from this "jalousie qui me rendit, *autrefois,* si incommode" (my emphasis).

Jealousy seems to structure the tensions in this family in several ways which might be clarified by looking at some common definitions of this word:

> JALOUSIE 1. *Vx.* Attachement vif et ombrageux. 2. *Mod.* Sentiment mauvais qu'on éprouve en voyant un autre jouir d'un avantage qu'on ne possède pas ou qu'on désirerait posséder exclusivement.... (*Petit Robert* 1040)

The distinction made in the second definition of jealousy quoted here is significant. Jealousy can be the desire to possess what one does not have *or* it can be the desire to possess this thing or person exclusively. In these stories it is the second of these which is addressed explicitly: children and father vie for the mother, the mother suffers from rivalry for her son's affection. However, it could be that the first part of this definition is equally important: jealousy could derive from sexual taboos in the family. The mother's jealousy could be based on the fact that she is forbidden a sexual relationship with her son. The daughter's jealousy of her father would thus follow this pattern: it is the sexual desire and pleasure in her parents' relationship which would be missing in her own relationship with her mother. It is not necessary that these desires be consciously admitted in order to create tensions in the family. The father's almost total exclusion from this text could be due to the fact that his presence interferes with the mother-daughter bond that Colette is creating. It is as though Colette is rewriting the "family romance" to suit her preferences. There is very little reference in these texts to Sido's desire for her husband; rather, she is responsible for him as she is for her children. "Dans la grappe pendue à ses flancs, à ses bras, mon père pesait comme nous, et ne nous soutenait guère" (*Sido* 50).

In *Sido* jealousy is more prominent than in the other texts, but the focus has shifted to an examination of rivalry between women for women.

> — Si longtemps chez Adrienne?
> Pas un mot de plus, mais quel accent! Tant de clairvoyance et de jalousie en "Sido", tant de confusion en moi refroidirent, à mesure que je grandissais, l'amitié des deux femmes....Il m'a fallu beaucoup de temps pour que j'associasse un gênant souvenir, une certaine chaleur de coeur, la déformation féerique d'un être et de sa demeure, à l'idée d'une première séduction. (30)

It is with this story that Colette finishes the "Sido" section of this text, thus it is prominently placed. The effect is as if to emphasize her importance to her mother. Adrienne Saint-Alban is only mentioned on one other occasion in these texts; in each case it is noted that she had briefly nursed the baby Gabrielle when the mothers exchanged their infants. The focus is on this breast that is both maternal and non-maternal as it is *a* mother's breast but not *the* mother's:

> [J]'avais goûté, nourrissonne, au lait de sa gorge abondante et bistrée, un jour que par jeu ma mère tendait son sein blanc à un petit Saint-Alban de mon âge. (*Maison* 108)

The second reference is more indicative of the merging of the maternal and the sexual:

> Parfois Adrienne m'interpellait en riant : 'Toi que j'ai nourrie de mon lait!...' Je rougissais si follement que ma mère fronçait les sourcils, et cherchait sur mon visage la cause de ma rougeur. Comment dérober à ce lucide regard, gris de lame et menaçant, l'image qui me tourmentait : le sein brun d'Adrienne et sa cime violette et dure... (*Sido* 29–30)

As in the story "Les deux chattes," the maternal breast is assimilated in these passages to seduction. Colette does not elaborate further on this "first seduction" but it is clear that it began with the breast offered to the baby Gabrielle. It is as though the categories that are maintained by the incest taboo cannot be breached without "contamination" of maternal purity by Eros: once a baby is suckled by (an)other not the (m)other, "l'un tétant l'autre, mêlés, heureux, gis[ant]...dans l'ombre" ("Les deux chattes"), the breast is the source of a seduction, a seduction that disturbs the distinction between sexual desire and maternal love.[11] However, in these two stories, as in the story of "La Toutouque" discussed earlier, the responsibility is shifted from the mother to another. Whether Colette is discussing her mother's desire or her desire for her mother, "Sido" is often displaced by someone less disturbing: a neighbor or a pet.

For although the role of seduction in familial relationships is significant in these texts, Sido is usually presented as innocent of these manipulations:

> Elle n'a jamais su qu'à chaque retour l'odeur de sa pelisse en ventre-de-gris, pénétrée d'un parfum châtain clair, féminin, chaste, éloigné des basses séductions axillaires, m'ôtait la parole et jusqu'à l'effusion. (*Sido* 7)

In this description we find an opposition that is fundamental to the representation of women in these texts: chastity versus seduction. Colette's use of adjectives such as "pure" or "chaste" when describing her mother is almost insistant and results in distancing "Sido" from desire. Certainly she is married and loves her husband but the impression often given is that this love is not noticeably different from her love for her children.[12] When Colette addresses her mother as "toi que je voulais pure de mes crimes ordinaires," it would seem that her concern is not only to show her mother's usual distance from jealousy as was suggested earlier, but also to affirm that it is her mother's distance from desire which generally protects her from being dominated (as are Colette and her father) by this emotion.

There is, however, another important point in the passage just quoted which is the depth of the child's emotion at her mother's return, at her mother's smell: she is, in a sense, seduced. Yet this seduction is arrived at through her mother's chaste distance ("éloigné des basses séductions") from passion. The emphasis on seduction gives female desire an ambivalent status in these stories of Colette's family. When women in these texts desire men it seems that their fury transforms them in such a way that mother becomes other, unknowable and frightening. "Sido's" desire is, if not suppressed, directed away from the father. Moreover, the woman-to-woman connection in these stories often gives the men involved secondary status: they are objects to be fought over or cared for but without the profound emotional connection that women supply. In all of these texts the references to jealousy show a troubled area where sexuality and family bonds, particularly maternal love, are mixed. This presentation of her childhood could be read as the story of Colette's jealousy. In these texts desire for men is either disfiguring or it is discounted. By this treatment of heterosexual desire, she keeps the mother for herself. Returning to Irigaray's image of a "mère-vierge," an image which is so central in our culture, we can see that Colette is also participating in a way in this restriction of the mother's *jouissance.*

In *La maison de Claudine,* Colette primarily shows competitive jealousy between females; she either treats it lightly as in her mother's entertaining monologue, or she distances it by showing its effects among animals. In *La naissance du jour,* jealousy is treated more seriously: it seems to be Sido's only flaw and it is presented as a major failing in Colette's father and one that she is not happy to have inherited from him. It is in *Sido* that this emotion is given the most prominence: Sido's rivalry with Adrienne for Gabrielle, the daughter's desire to be the exclusive recipient of her mother's attention, the father's desire for his wife's undivided love.[13] A progression can be seen in the treatment of jealousy: in each text it is used to demonstrate more of the uncertainties and the imbalances that lie beneath the surface of any family, no matter how loving.

The motifs of mourning and jealousy in these texts can be contrasted: while the theme of mourning worked toward a resolution and was not very significant in the third text, jealousy becomes increasingly important. In each text the problems and unease associated with this emotion are more explicitly addressed. I would suggest that as Colette acquires a distance from her mother that allows her to see Sido as a peer and thus finish mourning her, it also allows her to evaluate and portray family complexities with less idealism. In *Sido* family relationships, like other relationships, are hardly ever equal; rather, they are balances between various needs and claims that are always shifting.

An examination of these motifs helps to evaluate in a different manner the mother-daughter relationship that is so central to an understanding of Colette's work. Through this analysis we have seen that problems of identity are explored and at least partially resolved through mourning; however, the questions arising from the eroticism which can exist in the mother-daughter relationship are not so easily laid to rest. Freud theorized three resolutions to this important bond: lesbianism, frigidity, or "normal" heterosexuality. Colette finds a different way of living with her continued attachment. In her writing she returns to the mother's body. The "mémoire ouverte" that I described at the beginning of this chapter as an atemporal circularity common to proponents of *écriture féminine* and also found in Colette's work is phrased in *La naissance du jour* as "le chemin du retour" (24). However, this return is problematized: it is necessary to acknowledge the changes that have taken place since this first loss. Especially in *La naissance du jour,* Colette addresses her sense of unworthiness when comparing the adult that she has become to the child that she was and also when comparing herself to her mother. It is as though in this novel she mourns herself as well as the losses that she has experienced or is preparing to experience. Her reflection on the beginning of life requires an attention to its end. "Aurais-je atteint ici ce que l'on ne recommence point?" (24). The return to the mother's body involves a merging of identities that can be either comforting or frightening, recalling Irigaray's questions: "Est-ce que je ne suis pas morte aussi?" Even the mother's death does not always release a daughter to clearer self-knowledge. Even a daughter who loves her mother can still be troubled by the need for separation.

It is perhaps through her representation of jealousy that Colette finds a way of being merged with yet distinct from her mother. This emotion that she portrays as so important in her family both binds and separates those whom it affects. The desire to possess another could be seen as the desire to merge with the other while, precisely, being forced to acknowledge her otherness. Thus jealousy, while described as potentially dangerous, also has its place in Colette's life, as do many other aspects of human existence which she presents as neither positive nor negative, but both, and necessary.

The hidden mother

> Une des grandes banalités de l'existence, l'amour, se retire de la mienne. L'instinct maternel est une autre grande banalité. Sortie de là, nous nous apercevons que tout le reste est gai, varié, nombreux.
>
> *La naissance du jour*

La relation mère/fille, fille/mère constitue un noyau

extrêmement explosif dans nos sociétés.

Le corps-à-corps avec la mère

The views of the maternal as either banal or explosive in these two citations can be understood (as so much in the work of these two writers) as not truly opposed. What Colette seems to be criticizing in both sexual love and the maternal instinct is their predictability. I read her statement as a suggestion that we take love and the maternal out of their banal and commonly accepted definitions and re-examine them. In her portrayal of mother-child relations in these texts Colette strips away any possible banality by showing the complexity of these relations. As in her renunciation of "amour" in this text in which she shows that male-female relations can be varied and different once outside the battles of sexual passion, so she shows as well that the maternal is an entire range of actions, reactions, and feelings—not simply the patriarchally imposed cliché.

In its own way Colette's exploration of the mother-daughter bond is explosive in refusing reductive clichés. Any attempt to see this relation outside male fantasies is certain to be revolutionary in challenging our entire understanding of our culture. Even Colette's all-nurturing mother is not always what she might seem.

> Ma mère me retenait par le bout d'une de mes tresses, et son soudain visage sauvage, libre de toute contrainte, de charité, d'humanité, bondissait hors de son visage quotidien. (*Sido* 28)

This is the face of the Mother that has been hidden by a misogynistic and matricidal civilization. These sudden surges toward a liberty that leaves the mother almost unrecognizable are just as important, if not more, as the descriptions of the woman who is "bonne, ronde, humble devant l'ordinaire de sa vie." Colette's representations of the "feminine" are subversive in their refusal of "la loi du père."

She suggests that a woman's desire can create "une loi écrite par elle seule, pour elle seule." Independent yet together, merged yet different, Colette's representations of women are an eruption of the other in paternal discourse. "Sido" and "Colette"/"Gabrielle" together help to show the crevasses in the surface of patriarchal domination.

Notes

[1] Some examples of this are Erica Mendelson Eisinger and Mari Ward McCarty, eds., *Colette: The Woman, The Writer*; Susan D. Fraiman, "Shadow in the Garden: The Double Aspect of Motherhood in Colette"; Marianne Hirsch, *The Mother/Daughter Plot: Narrative, Psychoanalysis, Feminism*; Valérie Lastinger, "*La Naissance du jour*: la désintégration du 'moi' dans un roman de Colette"; Elaine Marks, *Colette*; Nancy K. Miller, "D'une solitude à l'autre: vers un intertexte féminin"; and Sylvie Tinter, "Sidonie Colette ou le temps de la mère." Two texts which I read after writing this chapter give admirable analyses of Colette's work which in some ways parallel mine: see Jerry Aline Flieger's *Colette and the Fantom Subject of Autobiography*, which has a much more extensively developed analysis of mourning in Colette's autobiographical texts, and Lynne Huffer's *Another Colette: The Question of Gendered Writing*, particularly the first two chapters, which focus on the role of both parents in Colette's work.

[2] The word "materrenelle" was coined by Hélène Cixous and discussed briefly by Domna Stanton in "Difference on Trial: A Critique of the Maternal Metaphor in Cixous, Irigaray, and Kristeva" in *The Poetics of Gender*, edited by Nancy K. Miller.

[3] I will use quotation marks around proper names whenever I think it particularly important to maintain an awareness of the fictionalizing of the character-persons in these texts.

[4] Marianne Hirsch's review essay "Mothers and Daughters" gives an excellent overview of writings on mother-daughter relations. For her discussion of feminist criticism treating the pre-oedipal see pages 204–11.

[5] In *Le corps-à-corps avec la mère*, pp. 29–30, Irigaray suggests that women situate themselves through "feminine" genealogies, both within the immediate family and in cultural history.

[6] Lynne Huffer and Nancy K. Miller discuss Colette's use of "Sido" as model, particularly in *La naissance du jour*.

[7] See also Jerry Aline Flieger's discussion of this story in

Colette and the Fantom Subject of Autobiography, pp. 137–38. Although Flieger and I have very similar readings of the two paragraphs quoted here, her emphasis on the use of comic effects, (her chapter cited here is called "Wit and the Work of Mourning") and the "legacy of laughter" that is part of Colette's heritage from her mother is somewhat different from my focus on an "indifferentiation" of categories that are more typically seen as polarized.

[8]See the *Dossier* at the end of the edition cited of *La naissance du jour* for Sido's actual letters.

[9]Sido's metamorphosis (from blackbird back to mother) is emphasized in the French at the lexical level: to change from *merle* to *mère* one must remove an "l" (pronounced as is the word *aile*, "wing" in French). With the loss of a wing she is earthbound. Another possibility, suggested to me by Mary Lydon, is that the "l" might be thought of as *elle*, meaning "she," implying perhaps that the role of mother could involve a loss of femininity.

[10]These two sources of denial could of course be combined in an adult male who might want to control female sexuality both as husband and as son.

[11]Also see Nicole Ward Jouve's discussion of this passage in *Colette*, pp. 120–122.

[12]Elaine Marks in *Colette* pp. 217–219 talks about the importance of the word "pure" in Colette's work. She suggests that it refers "to a privileged domain or state, reserved only for a few, free from anything extraneous to the ruling passion." Marks goes on to say that for Sido this ruling passion concerns "the daily adventures of her house, her garden and her village." I believe that this is in agreement with my view of the presentation of "Sido" as loving but not desiring.

[13]Although Colette mentions that her father's possessive jealousy in some ways included his children as rivals, she does not depict any situations involving this competition; therefore, although referring to this rivalry, I have not elaborated upon it.

Chapter III

Complicity and Silence
in *Mémoires d'une jeune fille rangée* and *Une mort très douce*

D'ordinaire je pensais à elle avec indifférence. Pourtant, dans mon sommeil — alors que mon père apparaissait très rarement et d'une manière anodine — elle jouait souvent le rôle essentiel: elle se confondait avec Sartre, et nous étions heureuses ensemble. Et puis le rêve tournait au cauchemar : pourquoi habitais-je de nouveau avec elle? comment étais-je retombée sous sa coupe? Notre relation ancienne survivait donc en moi sous sa double figure: une dépendance chérie et détestée.

Une mort très douce

The dual character of the mother-daughter relationship that is brought out in this important passage from Simone de Beauvoir's book on her mother's death is an essential aspect of Beauvoir's representation of her mother. This duality is also in evidence in the other autobiographical text in which Beauvoir speaks at length about her mother: *Mémoires d'une jeune fille rangée*. The two texts will be used in this chapter to address an important aspect of women's self-representations: the difficulties of the differentiation of the self from the mother. In order to examine the problem of mother-daughter differentiation I will explore the ambivalence in Simone de Beauvoir's representation of her mother, and the connections between this ambivalence and her view of her own "femininity." I believe that her representation of mother as Other played an important role in her project of self-representation and influenced her manner of presenting difference or separation between men and women, self and others.

The passage quoted at the beginning of this chapter shows a

range of oppositional terms used to describe this writer's feelings for her mother: her general indifference is juxtaposed to her mother's essential place in her dream, her dependence is both loved and hated, the happy dream becomes a nightmare. The description of Françoise de Beauvoir in *Mémoires d'une jeune fille rangée* and *Une mort très douce* is also often established in terms of juxtapositions: she is not what her husband is, she is the opposite of her daughter. The character "Françoise de Beauvoir" thus shapes the existence of the daughter through opposition: by locating who Simone de Beauvoir *is not*, "Françoise de Beauvoir" gives an identity to the daughter. The oppositional framework often seems to be the basis of Beauvoir's view of self in the world.

The oppositions that Simone de Beauvoir establishes in the *Mémoires* between her father and her mother, between masculine and feminine roles, are clearly important to this writer.

> [J]e m'habituai à considérer que ma vie intellectuelle — incarnée par mon père — et ma vie spirituelle — dirigée par ma mère — étaient deux domaines radicalement hétérogènes, entre lesquels ne pouvait se produire aucune interférence. La sainteté était d'un autre ordre que l'intelligence; et les choses humaines — culture, politique, affaires, usages et coutumes — ne relevaient pas de la religion. (*Mémoires* 57)

Certain critics have already noted that during her life Beauvoir more frequently chose the "masculine" side of the oppositions that she establishes in these texts: mother/father, emotion/intellect, weakness/strength, religion/sexuality, sexuality/intellect.[1] For Beauvoir the mother represents emotion, weakness, religion, and a sexuality which is equated to a lack of control. The father represents intellect, power, and a sexuality which is liberating and confers mastery, both over his own life and over women. Both the life and work of Simone de Beauvoir indicate the choice that she made between these two models. Beginning with her adolescence when her father tells her that she has the brains of a man, she devotes herself to transcending her female body, to being unique, not like other women (not Other), to allying herself with men. This is not to say that she tried to deny her sex. Yet it is clear in much of her work that her attitude toward her status as a woman among men was ambivalent. The reader often has the impression that Beauvoir is assuming that the role of men in our society is the better one, and that if women were free they would be like men.

In addition to representing her oppositional relation to her mother, Simone de Beauvoir finds it important to enunciate the oppositions within her mother. "Françoise de Beauvoir" signifies the Other for her daughter, yet an Other who is herself divided.

> Penser contre soi est souvent fécond; mais ma mère, c'est une autre histoire : elle a vécu contre elle-même. Riche d'appétits, elle a employé toute son énergie à les refouler et elle a subi ce reniement dans la colère. Dans son enfance, on a comprimé son corps, son coeur, son esprit, sous un harnachement de principes et d'interdits. On lui a appris à serrer elle-même étroitement ses sangles. En elle subsistait une femme de sang et de feu : mais contrefaite, mutilée, et étrangère à soi. (*Mort* 60–61)

These images of self-mutilation are central in Simone de Beauvoir's description of her mother and an underlying theme of *Une mort très douce* is the violation, physical and psychical, of women in our society. Yet we must bring together, as Beauvoir does not, these images of the mother with images of the writer herself as split into <<un coeur de femme, un cerveau d'homme>> (*Mémoires* 419). It seems that living against oneself is an experience that the daughter has shared with the mother, although certainly in very different ways: Françoise de Beauvoir, in her role of bourgeois housewife, experienced oppression differently from Simone de Beauvoir, as a woman intellectual in an androcentric society. Yet both situations could be said to have turned the woman against herself for her own survival. Beauvoir can describe this problem in her mother's life, yet does not enunciate its existence in her own, and thus I would suggest participates to a certain extent in the misogynistic ideology of our culture by denying the similarities between her mother and herself. In a woman's representation of the mother as Other it is sometimes difficult to distinguish between the individuation which is necessary to her survival and a repudiation of her connection to the maternal body. Living in a culture which in many ways debases or even represses the maternal figure, it becomes very difficult for the daughter herself to understand her fear of this connection.

Complicity

> Dans une fille, la mère ne salue pas un membre de la caste élue : elle y cherche son double. Elle projette en elle toute l'ambiguïté de son rapport à soi : et quand s'affirme l'altérité de cet *alter ego*, elle se sent trahie.
>
> Le deuxième sexe

> De l'archaïsme de la relation pré-objectale, de la violence immémoriale avec laquelle un corps se sépare d'un autre pour être, l'abjection conserve cette nuit où se perd le contour de la chose signifiée...Gêne, malaise, vertige de cette ambiguïté qui, par la violence d'une révolte *contre*, délimite un espace à partir de quoi surgissent des signes, des objets.
>
> Pouvoirs de l'horreur

The two motifs of complicity and silence which I have chosen to examine in Simone de Beauvoir's writings on her mother will help me to elucidate further the question of the different ways in which women need to distinguish themselves from their mothers. I believe that these two motifs will show the interconnections between the socially imposed denial of the mother and the necessary individuation that must occur between mother and child. The two motifs represent a possible internalization of male dominance and misogyny. Women are not only silenced by men, they silence themselves and they silence other women. Equally, the subversion of male authority which is implied by women's loyalty to other women requires that any closeness between them is seen negatively as complicity, both by men and by the women themselves. These two aspects of androcentric oppression appear in Beauvoir's work in such a way as to give an indication of her own ambivalence toward what is categorized as the "feminine." They circumscribe her relation to her mother, demonstrating not only men's oppression of women but women's oppression of themselves, and of other women.

In my analysis of what I am calling a fear of a mother-daughter complicity in these texts I would like to discuss several causes for the repression of women's connections to other women. I believe that the fear of closeness to the mother is related to the two interdependent domains of the psyche and the society. For the mother-child relation is important not only for its place in a socially constructed hierarchy but also because of the role of the mother in the earliest phases of personality development. The citations with which I began this section each address, although very differently, the "ambiguity" of the mother-child relation (in Beauvoir's text it is specifically the mother-daughter relation) and the need for the child to struggle against the loss of self implicit in this ambiguity.

My discussion of this aspect of the mother-daughter relation is informed by two texts of Julia Kristeva: *Pouvoirs de l'horreur* and *Histoires d'amour*. Rather than theorizing the pre-oedipal as an idyllic merging of mother and infant, in these texts Kristeva sees this as a frightening period when the infant is torn between various strong forces: the needs for closeness and protection are juxtaposed to the need for separation that exists even before the ego is clearly formed. A key concept in Kristeva's formulation of this phase is that of abjection.[2] She defines the abject as a process which is part of the struggle for individuation that occurs in the mother-child relation even before the mirror phase, before any division is perceived between subject and object. Kristeva suggests that even before these crucial events there is a need to establish borders between the "self" and the maternal.

> L'abject nous confronte...et cette fois dans notre archéologie personnelle, à nos tentatives les plus anciennes de nous démarquer de l'entité *maternelle* avant même que d'exister en dehors d'elle grâce à l'autonomie du langage. (*Pouvoirs de l'horreur* 20)

These borders are necessary to the survival of what could be called a pre-ego and thus a sense of delineation, division, and separation is one of the very first human requirements. A lack of boundaries is perhaps the source of the first feelings of horror that the human being experiences. It is the ambiguous—the confused or blurred—which causes the nauseated repulsion which is a part of abjection. The passage just quoted also recalls the connection between separation from the mother and language acquisition. It would seem that women's autobiographical projects could be linked to this struggle: although language establishes identity for both men and women, the separation process between mother and daughter seems to extend throughout the daughter's life. The autobiographical text can reflect the place of language as a barrier to mother-daughter merging.

Whether taking place at this beginning of personal prehistory, or erupting in the adult psyche, the abject necessarily involves a perception that is oppositional. It is only through the establishment of distinct antithetical categories that the pre-ego can feel unified. In other words, the need for existence outside the overwhelming maternal presence is answered by a movement toward dichotomy.

> Celui par lequel l'abject existe est donc un *jeté* qui (se) place, (se) sépare, (se) situe et donc *erre,* au lieu de se reconnaître, de désirer, d'appartenir ou de refuser....Forcément dichotomique, quelque peu manichéen, il divise, exclut et, sans à proprement parler vouloir connaître ses abjections, ne les ignore nullement. (*Pouvoirs* 15)

This emphasis on separation and polarization is an aspect of Occidental thinking which is so embedded in our ideologies that it has rarely been questioned or analyzed. Since the beginning of Western civilization we have accepted essential divisions such as Good and Evil, Superior and Inferior, Self and Other, to name a few of these important binaries. Kristeva's description of abjection locates at least part of the cause of these polarized notions of being in the first months of human life.

It is also important to note Kristeva's use of the Freudian concept of identification which could be seen as a complement to the concept of abjection. Whereas abjection is a process of separation, identification also takes place in prehistory yet is a merging. "Je m'identifie non pas avec un objet, mais à ce qui se propose à moi comme modèle" (*Histoires d'amour* 36). Primary identification also takes place before the subject-object awareness that occurs with the mirror phase.

Although the most frequent images of the mother-daughter relation in Simone de Beauvoir's texts emphasize differentiation, I believe that the rare instances of mother-daughter merging are equally important. Kristeva's examination of the two seemingly opposed movements of abjection and identification can be used to articulate the varied responses to the mother that are found in *Mémoires d'une jeune fille rangée* and *Une mort très douce*. Beauvoir's view of masculine and feminine as well as of herself and her mother seems to be based on dichotomization. The concepts of abjection and identification help to elucidate the connections between the formation of the individual and the ways in which women's relations to women are structured in our society.

The passages in which Simone de Beauvoir describes her fear of a closeness or complicity between herself and her mother are notable for an almost inexplicable force in the daughter's need for separation.

> Si elle m'avait convaincue de mensonge, j'aurais ressenti son scandale plus vivement que ma honte : l'idée m'en était si intolérable que je disais toujours la vérité. (*Mémoires* 56)
> Pour moi, l'existence des filles-mères était un fait objectif qui ne m'incommodait pas plus que celle des antipodes : mais la

connaissance que j'en avais deviendrait, à travers la conscience
de ma mère, un scandale qui nous souillerait toutes deux.
(*Mémoires* 154)

These citations show a complicated fear of intimacy with the mother, an association of guilt and unbearable closeness which almost seems exaggerated. The reader is struck by the force of the words "intolérable," "souillerait," and "scandale." There is a sense of horror at what could happen: if she admitted her guilt to her mother, both women would be in a situation unbearably intimate and shameful, a situation which is almost unspeakable. The reader is left with the idea of a complicity which would contaminate both women if it were acknowledged, yet the source of this fear is vague.

Simone de Beauvoir often refers to her desire for a closeness or complicity with her father: "[J]e me persuadai qu'une silencieuse alliance existait entre lui et moi" (*Mémoires* 150). However, it appears that there would be something intolerable or scandalous in an intimacy with her mother. The notion of guilt shared between women can be found everywhere in our culture, as we see in the curse upon Eve in the Bible which tells us that women are responsible for the existence of sin in the world. We could thus explain Beauvoir's repulsion as a refusal to share in the feminine destiny. Yet this seems an inadequate explanation of her horror.

In the passages in which Beauvoir recoils from intimacy we find the imposition of a distance necessary for her separation from the mother. What can be seen in the pages describing her mother and their relationship is an attempt to split this figure into positive and negative aspects, as well as a repeated enunciation of the split (the differences) between mother and daughter. Beauvoir's need for difference seems always to lead to opposition. The maternal body, in itself a signifying system, impels Simone de Beauvoir to write her distance from this body, to signify her self.[3] The need to signify separation reveals itself in her texts through the emphasis on polarization. In this way the unlike becomes conflated with the antithetical.

Returning to the passage on unwed mothers quoted above, we

should note the word that she chooses as having the same neutral value as a "fait objectif" is "antipodes." By her choice of a word that signifies things that are exactly opposed, she is again indicating her reliance on binary oppositions as the basis of her understanding of existence. For Beauvoir things are unquestioned in their opposition. This is her reference point in her view of her family, herself, and the world.

Beauvoir's confrontation with the sight of the naked body of her mother also causes extreme discomfort:

> Voir le sexe de ma mère: ça m'avait fait un choc. Aucun corps n'existait moins pour moi — n'existait davantage. Enfant, je l'avais chéri; adolescente, il m'avait inspiré une répulsion inquiète; c'est classique; et je trouvai normal qu'il eût conservé ce double caractère répugnant et sacré: un tabou. Tout de même, je m'étonnai de la violence de mon déplaisir.
> (*Mort* 27)

This "répulsion inquiète" and "la violence de [son] déplaisir" recall the passages that we have just examined in which she speaks of her fear of shared shame or guilt with her mother. Certainly her reactions to this moment of confrontation with the body that gave birth to her would be overdetermined. Yet this does not necessarily explain the violence of her discomfort. Once again we find a reference to a "double caractère" embodied by the mother. The passage is constructed around a series of oppositions: the presence or absence of the maternal body are contrasted, love is opposed to repulsion, the sacred and repellant nature of the taboo is noted. However this time the context clearly references an event which is fundamental in psychoanalytic theory: the view of the mother's genitals.

Freud tells us that the view of the mother's lack of penis leads to hatred on the daughter's part, and a resentment from which she might not ever recover. It is interesting that Simone de Beauvoir allows herself to invoke this tradition yet does not explicitly confront or address it. Indeed her relation to psychoanalytic theory is another site of ambivalence in her writings, perhaps even echoing her ambivalence to her mother. If we posit the science of psychoanalysis as based on the explanation of the relationship to the mother, these two areas of ambivalence in Beauvoir's writing would understandably be linked. Simone de Beauvoir's objection to psychoanalytic theories seems to have been based on her suspicion of any determinism in the view of a human life. When she portrays her own formative years, she insists on her ability to shape herself despite parental and social influences. Yet it would seem that by her acceptance of the "taboo," she is also accepting some of the views of the role of the mother's body in our culture as it has been theorized by Freud and his followers. In this way she shifts the responsibility for her discomfort onto her cultural formation and thus does not have to examine the complex and contradictory feelings of her particular relation to her mother.

She also takes it upon herself to ascribe the same feelings of repulsion to her sister: "[P]endant toute l'anesthésie Poupette avait tenu la main de maman, et j'imaginais quelle épreuve ç'avait été pour elle de voir tout nu ce vieux corps ravagé qui était le corps de sa mère" (*Mort* 41–42). It is perhaps true that it was difficult for Poupette to see her mother naked and vulnerable, but it almost seems as though Simone de Beauvoir is attempting to justify her own response by sharing it with her sister.

Although *Une mort très douce* shows, for the most part, the differences between Simone de Beauvoir and her mother, there are several important passages in which the daughter-mother boundaries seem to dissolve. One is the dream sequence which I quoted at the beginning of this chapter, another is when Beauvoir tells Sartre of her sorrow for her mother:

> Je parlai à Sartre de la bouche de ma mère, telle que je l'avais vue le matin...[e]t ma propre bouche, m'a-t-il dit, ne m'obéissait plus : j'avais posé celle de maman sur mon visage et j'en imitais malgré moi les mimiques. (43-4)

This description evokes the horror that comes from the dissolution of self into other. In abjection there is a movement which is simultaneously attraction and repulsion, a movement towards the symbiosis of the pre-oedipal phase yet at the same time away from the horrifying loss of identity. In this passage Simone de Beauvoir identifies herself so strongly with her mother that she seems to lose control of her body, giving it over to another. It is as though her personality splits in two. The ambivalent status of her own will and her own desires is indicated by the pronouns in this passage: "ma propre bouche...ne *m'obéissait*," "*j'*avais posé celle de maman sur mon visage," "*j'*en imitais malgré *moi*." The split in the narrator can be seen in the pronouns which show Beauvoir as both subject and object of her physical reactions. This is not a mind/body split, rather, it is a self/self split in which the "je" and the "moi" of the final line of this citation seem to be separated. The eeriness of this passage is emphasized by the fact that it is another, Sartre, who tells Beauvoir what is happening to her, as though she is so distanced from herself that another can translate her relation to her own body. The description of Beauvoir's mouth ends with another image of mother-daughter merging: "Toute [la personne de ma mère], toute son existence s'y matérialisaient et la compassion me déchirait" (44). Simone de Beauvoir is at this moment the embodiment of both mother and daughter but this tears her apart: the alternating movements of abjection and identification divide her.[4]

The motif of complicity in *Mémoires d'une jeune fille rangée* and *Une mort très douce* reveals in what ways Simone de Beauvoir's need to enunciate her differences from and connections to her mother is structured by the psychological and social formation of women in our culture, and precisely how difficult it is to separate psyche from society in an analysis of the mother-daughter relation. The fear of closeness to the mother that can be seen throughout these two texts is clearly related both to the lower status of women in her society, and to a need to ascertain her own independent existence, to affirm her own life despite her mother's death. The maternal body signifies both the power of the mother-child connection and the powerlessness of the female body in our culture. This ambiguity shapes the representation of the mother in these texts in such a way that the writer vacillates between two needs: to reject the mother and to mourn her loss.

Silence

> Cette aptitude à passer sous silence des événements que pourtant je ressentais assez vivement pour ne jamais les oublier, est un des traits qui me frappent le plus quand je me remémore mes premières années.
>
> *Mémoires d'une jeune fille rangée*

An analysis of the motif of silence in these texts must begin by acknowledging that Beauvoir's work was a continual struggle against the silencing of women which operates in our culture in various ways: women are not supposed to express themselves as much as men (like children they should be seen and not heard), and female things (the female body, female sexuality) are not suitable topics of discourse.[5] It would seem that this writer struggled against what is at least a double repression: as a woman who spoke of women she challenged the sexist proscriptions of her society on several levels simultaneously. Indeed, she was criticized for speaking "too much" and always about subjects of controversy.[6] However the texts in which she speaks of her mother are particularly important in that she breaks the silence imposed on women by speaking of the person who is the most directly responsible for this silencing in her life and thus indirectly addresses the social structures which make the mother responsible. In both of these texts she challenges her mother's attempted imposition of silence, in her roles of model and of teacher.

Yet there are moments in *Mémoires d'une jeune fille rangée* and *Une mort très douce* where it seems as though it is the writer herself who is imposing silence—on herself or others—and these moments are often related to a mother-daughter identification which is difficult for Simone de Beauvoir to acknowledge. The psychoanalytic definition of identification shows that, like abjection, it is based on two somewhat contradictory impulses: the need for distancing as well as the desire to merge.

> Freud montre...que ces identifications forment une structure complexe dans la mesure où le père et la mère sont chacun à la fois objet d'amour et de rivalité. Il est d'ailleurs probable que cette présence d'une ambivalence à l'égard de l'objet est essentielle à la constitution de toute identification. (Laplanche and Pontalis 189)

There are therefore various issues involved in mother-daughter identification. It is possible that an individual might not want to acknowledge identification because of a socially constructed need for distance from an other who is seen as inferior. Yet it is also the case that identification in itself leads to ambivalent feelings in the individual which would increase the difficulties of acknowledging the connection. In Simone de Beauvoir's descriptions of her mother's life and its influence on her own life, we can see love and rivalry expressed in various ways. In particular the rivalry could be founded on different notions of "femininity." Although forced to acknowledge similarities in their situations, Beauvoir wants to show that her assumption of the "feminine" role is very different from her mother's. My examination of silencing in these texts will include an attention to silence not only as an omission of a voice but also as a distanced narrative voice which attempts to conceal or deny identification. The objective tone of this narrative often helps Simone de Beauvoir to emphasize the differences between the victimization from which her mother suffered and the daughter's authorization of her own life.

In reading Simone de Beauvoir's portrayal of her mother we have the impression of a woman who is afraid to say what she feels and thinks—in her parents' home, in Parisian society, with her husband. Although there are two sides to the representation of Françoise de Beauvoir (there are also memories of a young, happy, loving *maman*), the side most often presented is that of a frustrated woman who has never felt herself free to express her emotions or desires; the restrictions and silencing become internalized as self-censorship, crippling her in her life and leading to an oppressive relationship with her daughters. Françoise de Beauvoir's self-repression creates a tense home atmosphere, where occasionally her unhappiness bursts out at her daughters, giving them confusing messages about their future as women. She tells them that they must be like her yet cannot help but show the futility of her life.

Beauvoir begins her account of her mother's life emphasizing her solitude: "A vingt ans, engoncée dans ses guimpes à baleines, habituée à réprimer ses élans et à enfouir dans le silence d'amers secrets, elle se sentait seule, et incomprise…" (*Mémoires* 51). This image of a woman who is restricted physically and psychologically is interesting because it shows a Françoise de Beauvoir—alone and misunderstood—with whom Simone de Beauvoir could probably have identified. However the narration of her mother's life seems distanced, objective rather than empathetic: "Enfance et jeunesse lui laissèrent au coeur un ressentiment qui ne se calma jamais tout à fait" (51). Beauvoir's ability as narrator to summarize and judge her mother's character diminishes any tendency to equate daughter and mother.

Although Simone de Beauvoir does not focus specifically on the importance of gender in her mother's upbringing, we can still see in the descriptions of the childhood of Françoise de Beauvoir that her experiences as a "dutiful daughter" (as her daughter was later to describe herself) were often limited and limiting. During her childhood and adolescence she felt undervalued by both parents. She was introduced to her future husband as a part of the marriage arrangements that were customary at that time yet often seemed particularly demeaning for women. Certainly, as Simone de Beauvoir points out, silencing is related not only to gender but to class as well. A young lady of the bourgeoisie of this era was not encouraged to voice her opinions or feelings. The mother, in passing on this repression to her daughter, was doing so partly in the interests of conforming to their social position.

Even if the Beauvoir marriage seems to have begun happily, it soon becomes obvious that the woman is the disadvantaged spouse. Her husband is free to turn away from her to other women and she is left to sit in silent anger, hurt, and frustration at home. Beauvoir emphasizes the impact that this rejection had on her mother.

> L'alliance passée à son doigt l'avait autorisée à connaître le plaisir; ses sens étaient devenus exigeants; à trente-cinq ans, dans la force de l'âge, il ne lui était plus permis de les assouvir. Elle continuait à dormir à côté de l'homme qu'elle aimait et qui ne couchait presque plus jamais avec elle : elle espérait, elle attendait, elle se consumait, en vain. (*Mort* 51)

Again it is possible to imagine an underlying identification with her mother. The passage just quoted begins with an unequivocal view of gender difference: "Je ne blâme pas mon père. *On sait assez que chez l'homme l'habitude tue le désir*" (my emphasis). This universalizing statement indicates the possibility that Simone de Beauvoir is retrospectively analyzing her mother's feelings through the screen of her own life experiences, her own beliefs about men and women. It is important to remember that Beauvoir was fifty when this text was published: an analysis of what her mother's feelings must have been in her mid-thirties could easily reflect what she herself might have experienced of masculine fidelity or lack thereof. Just as Colette's understanding of her mother's possible needs or desires seems to be reshaped over the course of time, with the knowledge and empathy that life experience would bring, so might Simone de Beauvoir's view of her mother's frustration be informed by her own life.

Yet this seeming identification is again balanced by a distancing in the narrative tone and technique. The process of writing an autobiographical account is, of course, always showing one perspective, that of the writer, yet autobiographers have choices in how much they attempt to show of the thoughts and feelings of others. Simone de Beauvoir extrapolates fairly often the interior processes of those around her. This omniscient perspective distances the writer from the characters that she creates in these texts. Her careful explanations of her own emotions and reactions make an interesting contrast to some of her characterizations of her mother: "[A] l'époque où sa vie affective était le plus tourmentée, elle n'avait ni doctrine, ni concepts, ni mots pour la rationaliser" (*Mort* 60). "Je m'attristais du contraste entre la vérité de son corps souffrant et les billevesées dont sa tête était farcie" (*Mort* 26). Beauvoir's use of "Françoise de Beauvoir" as a type or example of a certain sort of woman emphasizes the difference between the narrator and the character/mother.

When the mother's influence on her daughter is acknowledged, it is often shown to be negative:

> Ainsi vivions-nous, elle et moi, dans une sorte de symbiose, et sans m'appliquer à l'imiter, je fus modelée par elle. Elle m'inculqua le sens du devoir, ainsi que des consignes d'oubli et d'austérité. Mon père ne détestait pas se mettre en avant, mais j'appris de maman à m'effacer, à contrôler mon langage, à censurer mes désirs, à dire et à faire exactement ce qui devait être dit et fait. (*Mémoires* 56)

Love for the mother is used to turn the daughter against herself. The duality of Simone de Beauvoir's feelings again brings out the dual role of the mother in this family. It is the mother who must pass on to her daughter the repression from which she has suffered. As the instrument of a misogynistic ideology she is doubled as victim/oppressor. "Incapables de prévoir quel geste, quelle parole risquait de...déchaîner [sa censure], toute initiative comportait pour nous un danger : la prudence conseillait de se tenir coites" (*Mémoires* 55). Through tactics of unpredictable cruelty and humiliation she teaches her daughters the lessons that she learned: to live in silence, secrecy, and fear. This is an oppression that divides the victim: she mistrusts and fears her mother's anger yet still accepts that the mother's severity is due to her love and her need to form her daughter according to society's requirements.

Silence in this family becomes both oppression and protection.

"Aveux et commérages avaient quelque chose de furtif qui me répugnaient et je voulus que mes remparts fussent sans faille....Le silence entre nous est devenu tout à fait opaque" (*Mort* 95–96). The motif of silence in these texts articulates the complexity of the mother's role in the traditional family. As both oppressed and instrument of oppression the mother elicits pity and resentment, contempt and fear from her daughter.

Crucially important in both *Mémoires d'une jeune fille rangée* and *Une mort très douce* is the question of maternal power, or, more accurately, the power struggle between mother and daughter. It cannot be said that power is always purely on one side or the other in the mother/child relation, as each has her own, yet in these two works we can see a reversal: in the *Mémoires* it is the mother who directs Simone's life, in *Une mort très douce* it is Simone who directs the end of her mother's life. This is true in several ways: she cares for her mother financially and in all practical details, she limits her mother's knowledge as to the reality of her situation, and she then tells her readers the "reality" of what happened. It is questionable whether Beauvoir is comfortable with the situation of being the more powerful; in fact it seems that the uneasy relationship that has existed for a long time between mother and daughter makes this responsibility even more awkward.

There is often a sense that the possibility of a confrontation between these two women is in some way frightening to each of them.

> J'ai décidé: <<Cette nuit, c'est moi qui dormirai ici.>> Maman a paru inquiète...Elle a ruminé; elle m'a regardée avec intensité: <<Toi, tu me fais peur.>>....Et j'étais aussi crispée qu'à vingt ans quand elle essayait — avec son ordinaire maladresse — de faire de l'intimité: <<Je sais que tu ne me trouves pas intelligente. Mais, en tout cas, c'est de moi que tu tiens ta vitalité, ça me fait plaisir.>> Sur ce dernier point, j'aurais de grand coeur abondé dans son sens; mais le début de sa phrase coupait mon élan. Ainsi nous paralysions-

nous mutuellement. C'est tout cela qu'elle avait voulu dire en m'enveloppant de son regard: <<Toi, tu me fais peur.>> (*Mort* 94, 98)

Even though she explains that it is the paralyzed silence of the two women that is frightening, one is left wondering what would be said if they attempted to speak in all honesty to each other. The reader does not have a sense that there are important secrets that need to be divulged, rather, that the fear is a result simply of a constraint that has been lived with for so long that the idea of an ending to this constraint is almost unimaginable, and frightening in itself.

In *Une mort très douce*, Simone de Beauvoir speaks of her discomfort when she imposes silence upon her mother to hide from her that she is dying. "Au moment où la vérité l'écrasait et où elle aurait eu besoin de s'en délivrer par des paroles, nous la condamnions au silence..." (93–94). Silence has an ambiguous and troubling place in this text. Although Beauvoir justifies her decision to conceal the truth from her mother, her discomfort with this power is obvious. At the same time, her decision to write about this experience is again exercising her power, but in a different way, by revealing the most personal details of the life and death of her mother. It would seem that in this way she is continuing her struggle against the repressed/repressive society personified by her mother, confronting the power against which she has fought her entire life.

However, it would be too easy to say that *Une mort très douce* is Simone de Beauvoir's revenge on her mother. In spite of the anger and distrust that she shows, she also reveals the pain that results from the estrangement between mother and daughter. At the end of this book she speaks of the change which has taken place in their relationship:

> Je m'étais attachée à cette moribonde. Tandis que nous parlions dans la pénombre, j'apaisais un vieux regret : je reprenais le dialogue brisé pendant mon adolescence et que nos divergences et notre ressemblance ne nous avaient jamais

permis de renouer. Et l'ancienne tendresse que j'avais crue tout à fait éteinte ressuscitait depuis qu'il lui était possible de se glisser dans des mots et des gestes simples. (109)

The text of *Une mort très douce* is thus presented as the result of a more open relationship and the end of silence between mother and daughter. There would seem to be two new communications: the reestablishment of a mother-daughter dialogue and the recounting of this which is the written text. Yet we must remember that all of this is a representation by the daughter and, in fact, the silence has been modified but not broken in that the daughter continues to censor what she says to her mother and the mother does not really speak. Beauvoir tries to show what her mother means to her, but what is lacking in this representation is a sense of the mother as subject. There is relatively little direct quoting of the mother in this text; rather, we have the daughter's pronouncements on what her mother must have thought or felt.

Simone de Beauvoir shows her mother as a victim both of society and of herself. Yet her relationship to her mother is not without its own potential for victimization. I would suggest that the silence has passed to another level: as Beauvoir succeeds in speaking more freely to her mother and of her mother she gives the appearance of an end to silencing. However the view of the mother has not really changed; the reversal of power and the death of the mother bring about a greater liberty but the presentation of their relationship is still incomplete. Mother and daughter have not learned to speak to each other; the daughter can only tell one side of the story. In fact, the silences that are written into this text, covering over some of the daughter's struggles with herself and her mother, continue the problems in the mother-daughter relationship even after the mother's death. The ambivalence in this relationship is too painful and complex to be resolved even by death. Even in the passage quoted above, a plurality "nos divergences" is opposed to a singularity "notre ressemblance." In this passage where she speaks with renewed tenderness, there is still a need to emphasize the differences between the two women and to discount the similarities.

Identification is both acknowledged and struggled against.

The compelling image of a screen at the end of *Une mort très douce* helps to articulate the various facets of the representation of power and silence in this relationship:

> [D]ans les salles communes, quand approche la dernière heure, on entoure d'un paravent le lit du moribond; il a vu ce paravent autour d'autres lits qui le lendemain étaient vides : il sait. (135–36)

Although it would seem that the daughter's ability to pay for a private room protected her mother from the knowledge of her death by sparing her the screen around the bed that is used in public wards, her protection involved a different sort of screen: by limiting her mother's information, she protected her, but in a way that could be seen as disempowering the mother. In addition, the daughter's text could be understood as a screen that conceals her mother's subjectivity from the reader. In as much as the representation of "Françoise de Beauvoir" must inevitably occult the actual person, her subjectivity is protected or obscured by her textualization.[7]

It is not possible to say what exactly took place in this relationship at the end of Françoise de Beauvoir's life for the character "Françoise de Beauvoir" obscures the relationship. Similarly to the way in which silence becomes a metaphor for the power that oppresses women in our society and which is passed from mother to daughter, "Françoise de Beauvoir" comes to signify something more than the mother of the narrator: she seems to represent the site of a struggle in Simone de Beauvoir which this writer cannot clearly describe but which she is continually trying to resolve. One division that is apparent in these texts could be expressed as the confrontation of the writer and the daughter. This writer represents her mother in such a way as to show the contradictions and the resulting self-destruction inherent in a woman's role. Yet the daughter's need to show herself as different from her mother causes her representation of the mother to alternate between sympathy and judgement.[8]

Indeed the oppositional framework that is inherent in my own comparison of the two texts is troubled by the shifts that take place in the representations of "Françoise de Beauvoir." The dominating and overemotional mother in the *Mémoires* is often shown as courageous and admirable in *Une mort très douce*. Neither doubled nor antithetical the two representations of this woman expose the weaknesses in Beauvoir's oppositional ontology. It could be that it is the mother-daughter relation which subverts Beauvoir's antithetical thinking, in that the two are shown to be both opposed and merged.

I would suggest that Beauvoir's presence at her mother's final illness in some ways opened her thinking to the possibility of a less polarized view of this person. The dream that she describes at the end of the book in which her mother merges with Sartre, although addressing a duality in their relationship, also suggests that some of her categorizations could be breaking down. "Pourtant dans mon sommeil...elle se confondait avec Sartre, et nous étions heureuses ensemble" (147). Even in this passage where she speaks of duality, there is a potential for another way of experiencing this bond—not as a dichotomy, but as a merging which still maintains differences. In merging Françoise de Beauvoir with Jean-Paul Sartre, Simone de Beauvoir's dream gives her mother the place in her life that she did not always acknowledge.

At the end of *Une mort très douce*, Beauvoir gives the impression that she has resolved certain problems that she had had with her mother. Yet the manner in which this resolution has been achieved is left somewhat vague; one wonders if it is necessary for the mother to die so that the child can be comfortable with their relationship. Reading this text it would seem that the daughter becomes free with this death, but it is not clear whether in the end she has really succeeded in seeing her mother as the subject of her own life rather than as the (m)Other in Simone de Beauvoir's life.

The divided mother

> Il y a ensuite cet autre abîme qui s'ouvre entre ce corps et ce qui a été son dedans : l'abîme entre la mère et l'enfant.
>
> "Héréthique de l'amour"

According to contemporary psychoanalytic theory, a representation of the mother is always a representation of the child's desire. Looking for the moving object of Beauvoir's desire in the midst of this triangle of daughter, mother, and "mother" is a complicated, perhaps futile endeavor. Yet between all of these O/others—Beauvoir's existentialist Other which is so often represented by Woman, Lacan's Other as complete repository of Truth and Presence, and Lacan's *autre* (petit a) as an endless diacritical movement of desire—Simone de Beauvoir's "mother" shifts. Certainly the mother is the first representative of both the Other and *autre* of Lacan: not only is she the first object of desire but she is also the first signifier of Truth and Presence to the infant. In a sense, "Françoise de Beauvoir" begins to seem almost as unstable a signifier as is *je* in Lacanian theoretics: she is split, and her splitting continually destabilizes notions of identity. The splitting of the mother is used in *Mémoires d'une jeune fille rangée* and *Une mort très douce* to disrupt the sense of self that so often seems unquestioned in Beauvoir's writings. The role of the mother in these texts can be read as a symptom signifying loss of self that is trying to resolve itself in writing but is irresolvable.

In this sense, the mother as metaphor/symptom in Beauvoir's texts is very elusive, her role constantly shifting. What this notion of symptom does for us, however, is to articulate another opposition —Françoise de Beauvoir versus "Françoise de Beauvoir." These opposed figures—that of the woman who lived and died, who helped to shape Beauvoir's sense of herself as a person and as a woman, and that of the literary creation that is used as either background or contrast in Beauvoir's self-explication—both represent, in all of their power to disturb and disrupt, a problem that is crucial to the projects of feminist movements. Women are confronting their fear of becoming their mothers (a fear that is often so unquestioned that it is a commonplace) not only to begin to actualize true solidarity with other women, but to come to understand the importance (and elusiveness) of the concept of difference. If difference from our mothers were something that we did not feel that we had to fight for, as if in a life and death struggle, we could unseat this concept from its hegemony in our understanding of the notion of self. With this proposal I am not, I hope, falling back into what has been called indifference, rather, I am wondering if difference could be seen as something other than Othering, other than the foundation of phallological binary thinking.[9] It seems possible that difference could be somewhere in between indifference and polarization.

This attempted collapsing of binary categories is extremely useful to a discussion of Simone de Beauvoir's work. If she can be seen as someone in between these clearcut categories on which she so often relies, it can help our understanding of the tremendous influence that she had, not only on the women's movement, but on twentieth-century thinking in many areas. We could not only see her as somewhere in between her representation of the paternal and of the maternal, of "masculine" and "feminine" categories, we could also see her as somewhere in between mother and daughter, for the moments of identification in her work suggest that these two are not always clearly distinguishable. In attempting to bring together, not as synthesis but as ambiguity, some of these divisions, we thus achieve a more complex view of this extremely complex person and writer.

Simone de Beauvoir made of her entire life an attempt to refuse the silencing that had so damaged her mother's life. She often succeeded. However she imposes silence on her mother and affirms her complicity with her father. The two motifs discussed in this chapter are intertwined, for complicity is often contingent on silence, indeed, it often seems to be based on leaving unspoken the things of which one is afraid or ashamed. In the case of Simone de Beauvoir and her mother, we see that the daughter feels a shame that she does not express directly concerning the ties between them. Her silence and complicity are interdependent: if she challenged one, the other would also be undone. In her adherence to an ideology which bases itself on binary oppositions Beauvoir enters into complicity with androcentrism. In this way she also succeeds in repressing her fear of becoming the double, or indifferentiated from her mother. In actuality, the division that she carries out on her mother is located within her as well: woman's body, man's head, feminist who distrusts what she perceives to be "femininity."

The motifs of complicity and silence help to show the struggle within this writer. Each shows an oppression that she must carry out on herself as well as on her mother. Both struggling against and complying with male domination Simone de Beauvoir shows us the ways in which women fight themselves in order to survive oppression. "Françoise de Beauvoir" represents the forces, both interior and exterior, that divide women from themselves and from other women.

Notes

[1] For examples of this type of criticism, see Carol Ascher, *Simone de Beauvoir: A Life of Freedom* or Mary Evans, "Views of Women and Men in the Work of Simone de Beauvoir," in *Critical Essays on Simone de Beauvoir*, edited by Elaine Marks.

[2] For a detailed explanation of Kristeva's thinking on the abject, see Mary Jacobus, "*Dora* and the Pregnant Madonna" in *Reading Woman: Essays in Feminist Criticism.*

[3] In *La révolution du langage poétique* Julia Kristeva relates the semiotic order (as opposed to the symbolic) to the maternal body.

[4] Nancy K. Miller, in "Autobiographical Deaths," has a reading of this passage that differs somewhat from mine. She suggests that Simone de Beauvoir's grief for her mother could also be related to the fact that she never had a child herself: "Perhaps, finally, threaded through these memoirs of another's dying is the story of a double loss. Beyond the lost mother...the memoirs invoke an evaded maternity. They record the autobiographical death of one's own making, and, as a result, the traces of a double mourning: *as if* for the child one never had, as if for all one would never be" (39).

[5] Sidonie Smith, in Chapter 2 of *A Poetics of Women's Autobiography: Marginality and the Fictions of Self-Representation*, gives a very good analysis of the historical silencing of women in our culture.

[6] Elaine Marks addresses this in "Transgressing the (In)cont(in)ent Boundaries: The Body in Decline" in *Yale French Studies* 72, "Simone de Beauvoir: Witness to a Century."

[7] It is also worth noting that Julia Kristeva describes primary narcissism, which comes into existence after the mother-child dyad is ended by the father's intervention, as a "screen over emptiness" on pages 31–35 of *Histoires d'amour*. Although she speaks of an *écran* rather than a *paravent*, this is still an interesting intersection between the two texts.

[8] Another source of tension in Beauvoir's description of her mother's death undoubtedly has to do with her focus on class: although as a woman Françoise de Beauvoir is less privileged, her

death is clearly made easier by her daughter's financial success. Yet even though this is the most evident point in the discussion of the screen which is placed around the beds in a public ward, I do not think that it precludes my reading.

[9] Luce Irigaray uses "indifference" in *Speculum de l'autre femme* to describe the way in which difference between men and women has been obscured by phallocentric thinking, positing women as the negative of men, rather than different.

Chapter IV

Orality and Specularity
in *Un barrage contre le Pacifique*, *L'Eden Cinéma*, *L'amant*, and *L'amant de la Chine du Nord*

> Elle avait eu tellement de malheurs que c'en était devenu un monstre au charme puissant et que ses enfants risquaient, pour la consoler de ses malheurs, de ne plus jamais la quitter, de se plier à ses volontés, de se laisser dévorer à leur tour par elle.
>
> *Un barrage contre le Pacifique*

    The ongoing work of Marguerite Duras continues to put into question the division between story and history. Some of her most recent texts interweave autobiography with fiction, telling the story of a young woman's childhood in French Indochina, the misery of her family, a relationship with a wealthy man. Although each of the four texts that I will discuss, *Un barrage contre le Pacifique*, *L'Eden Cinéma*, *L'amant*, and *L'amant de la Chine du Nord*, tells approximately the same story, each telling is a transformation of this ontogenetic tale.

    The young woman of these stories is called Suzanne in *Barrage* and *L'Eden Cinéma* ;[1] *Barrage* is a novel with third-person narration whereas *L'Eden Cinéma* is a play in which the two children, daughter and son, recount their story. In *L'amant* the young woman is referred to as "je," "elle," or by descriptive phrases: "la fille blanche," "la petite pute," and others. The text is presented as autobiography yet this play of pronouns unsettles any fixed categorization. In *L'amant de la Chine du Nord* she is described as "l'enfant" or "elle"; this text seems to be a blend of novel and filmscript.

    Although the mother, unlike the girl, is always referred to in the same way, her personality is transformed over the course of these texts. The abusive and callous figure of *Barrage* is more complex in

L'amant. Although she is still abusive, her madness is presented as at least a partial justification. In *L'amant de la Chine du Nord,* she is loving, lucid, often admirable. The wealthy suitor is transformed both in title—in the earlier works he is M. Jo, in the later texts he is simply called the lover—and in character. There is a progression throughout the texts in which he becomes stronger, more appealing, more desirable. The events of these stories are somewhat different as well. In the earlier texts there is no sexual relationship; the young woman is repulsed by M. Jo. In *L'amant* and *L'amant de la Chine du Nord,* the reciprocal passion of the child and her lover is a central aspect of the story.

Since each of these texts is a slightly different version of the same story, the reader is induced to abandon the problematic distinction between fiction and autobiography and to accept what could almost be called the superreality of this story: what is being recounted comes to acquire a truth which surpasses questions of verifiable history. Duras' preface to the text of *L'amant de la Chine du Nord* maintains this refusal of "history": "Je suis redevenue un écrivain de romans" (12). This would seem to suggest that the text of *L'amant de la Chine du Nord* is a novel, yet that does not clarify the status of *L'amant.* Any attempt to separate *L'amant* and *L'amant de la Chine du Nord* into "real autobiography" versus "fictionalized autobiography" would only make the distinction that is being imposed between the two more tenuous. The reader comes to see that textual reality is all that can ever be known.

In fact, it is the existence of these different versions which begins to destroy the story (at least as history) and to introduce the concept of legend, which expresses with greater fluidity the different levels at which Duras' narratives seem to be working.

> What ought to be read is a *legend*...until the 16th c. this meant a saint's life, but with the Reformation and the hostility to the Catholic Church the meaning changed to "something told as history that is really made up." (*Dictionary of Word Origins* 211)

Orality and Specularity

All three uses of the word "legend" are important to an analysis of Duras' work. The first, most basic sense is simply of a written text: this is problematized in the texts that I have chosen to study by an increasing attention to the cinematic, sometimes seemingly in opposition to the literary. The hagiographical aspect of this definition is intriguing in reference to a writer who changed her name from Marguerite Donnadieu ("gift to God"): although not a person who dedicated herself or her life to God, this is someone who offers herself up to public scrutiny, comparison, praise or condemnation. The third part of the definition foregrounds the often difficult distinction between fiction and history which is central to Duras' project.[2]

In the different versions of (her)story that are found in these texts, the creation of self through language is not only acknowledged but emphasized, particularly in the later texts. The shifting pronouns of *L'amant* are only one indication of a postmodern view of the individual as both faceted and fragmented, in many ways constructed by the view and the language of the other. The many blank spaces left in these texts, both typographically and through disjunctive syntax and plot structure, express silence and madness, the unconscious which is often disguised by a more teleologically organized discourse. The emphasis on the family drama is inextricably connected to a post-Freudian view of self, of the impact of the family on development.

> [L'histoire de ma famille] est le lieu au seuil de quoi le silence commence. Ce qui s'y passe c'est justement le silence, ce lent travail pour toute ma vie. Je suis encore là, devant ces enfants possédés, à la même distance du mystère. Je n'ai jamais écrit, croyant le faire, je n'ai jamais aimé, croyant aimer, je n'ai jamais rien fait qu'attendre devant la porte fermée. (*L'amant* 34)

In this passage it would seem that writing cannot be separated from earliest childhood memories. It could be that this image of the child waiting outside the closed door refers to the Freudian formulation of the family drama. Yet it is also important that the door, as a barrier to knowledge, becomes equated to the story of the family. Duras must react by telling and retelling her part of the story. What is hidden is not simply the parents and their sexuality, but also the articulation of the mortal violence, "cette histoire commune de ruine et de mort," which formed these four people: mother, daughter, sons. The mystery that holds the children before the door, that "possesses" them, also acts upon the reader of these texts, exercising a fascination which cannot always be clearly defined.

Duras' presentation of her family can thus be situated within both the Freudian understanding of the family, and the Lacanian emphasis on language as formative of all knowledge of self and other. In a sense, this is a deconstruction of the autobiographical project: instead of unveiling the self, Duras unveils the mechanisms of self-construction.

The two motifs which I have chosen as explicative of the mother-daughter relationship in Duras' work are closely linked to contemporary psychoanalytic theory. The first of these motifs is the theme of nourishment/orality which is emphasized in different ways in each of the texts.[3] The peasant children dying of hunger on the plain where the family has its concession, the mother's anxiety concerning the feeding of her children, the older brother's domination at the dinner table: all of these have a psychoanalytic significance as well as referring to the sociohistorical context. The second motif is the specularity which becomes more and more important in the development of these texts. The young woman is increasingly shaped by the look of others—society, men, family— and this specularization comes to dominate both her representation of her self to herself, and the representation of this character in the text. The reader is caught up in a web created by these overdetermining gazes and is forced to recognize her own participation in the specular economy. Once again this theme of women being looked at and looking at themselves is clearly involved with the sociohistorical and economic context, yet psychoanalytically based analyses of this attention to the woman's place in specularization must not be forgotten.

Both specularity and orality are connected to the infant's identification with the mother, the process through which the subject is constituted. Both are related to the confusion concerning the difference between self and other, and ambivalence toward the other. Both are involved in the process of separation from the mother. In these texts the connection to the mother is often linked to madness and the fear of being engulfed by the mother and/or by her insanity. One question that is possibly being asked over the course of these texts (and perhaps in everything that Duras has ever written) is the question of how a child can survive maternal madness. There are no definitive answers given in Duras' texts.

Luce Irigaray's theorization of specula(riza)tion is very useful in a reading of these works. Beginning with *Speculum de l'autre femme* and continuing in her more recent writings, she suggests that women have been used to mirror men to themselves, a role which excludes women as subjects in the specular economy and is responsible for what Irigaray calls "indifference." This formulation brings together at least two concepts, specularity and speculation (the latter meaning both a financial operation and a mental process), and relates them to the phallocentrism of our society. Irigaray suggests that dominance of the phallus in our culture is founded on the sight of women. It could also be said that speculation, both in its connotation of abstract visualization and in its relation to finance, places women in a submissive position. Mental imagery gives authority to sight over the other senses (as well as to the abstract over the concrete), financial speculation makes use of changing value for profit. Speculation thus could be understood as abstracting women from their relation to their own bodies for profit. Women become objects of commerce in their alienation from their bodies which is in part carried out by the male gaze.

It has been said that women are obsessed with their appearance; Irigaray helps us to see that appearance is all that women have been allowed to be. It is also the case that women come to perceive themselves only in terms of the male gaze: in some ways they only come into existence when seen, when desired, when objectified by a look of desire. Both objectification and passivity are imbricated in the conception of specula(riza)tion; Irigaray's concept helps us to understand that the role of passive object of the male gaze has been assigned to women since the beginning of our civilization.

Particularly in *Et l'une ne bouge pas sans l'autre*, Irigaray addresses the interwoven issues of mother as source of nourishment and as source of self-representation. The daughter's voice in this text complains of an overabundance of nourishment and a lack of reciprocity of gaze from a mother who seems to have no face, no representation. The daughter is stuffed with food in such a way that it seems that she is consuming her mother, yet what she requires is recognition, a gaze that will meet hers. She is filled with her mother and cannot receive acknowledgement of her own separate identity. If the mother is unrepresented to herself, she cannot provide the mirror that the child needs to begin to establish her own self-image. If the child is force-fed the mother's own substance, she will never be able to construct the necessary boundaries between them.

It is also important to note the connections between *écriture féminine* and *écriture durassienne*.[4] Irigaray's emphasis on fluidity, circularity, openness, and silence could almost be read as descriptive of Duras' texts. Irigaray's attention to language as the encoding of gender and her belief in "difference" as an important political position for women are, if not overtly addressed in Duras' work, at least echoed.[5] These metalinguistic formulations can be read together with Duras' "biomythography"[6] to give new access to each writer's work.

The theories of Julia Kristeva concerning the pre-oedipal attachment to the mother are also important to my understanding of Duras. Kristeva hypothesizes that a third term is crucial for a viable separation between mother and infant. Although she usually speaks of the father's intervention in the mother-child dyad as constitutive of a ternary relation, it is possible that this third term could be some other object of the mother's desire, anything that would convey to the infant that the desire of the mother is directed elsewhere. Kristeva believes that the lack of this intervening third results in psychosis; in some form the Name of the Father is necessary for individuation and sanity. Her description of "borderline" cases identifies what seems to be a linguistic disconnection from self in these cases. In other words, children who did not experience the third term intervention did not enter completely into the symbolic order and thus have a dysfunctional relationship to language. The increased gap between signifier and signified that Kristeva describes in borderline language also has an important place in much contemporary writing which by deliberately challenging the arbitrary connection of signifier and signified creates a language that on occasion seems to evoke pychosis.

Kristeva's notion of the semiotic is relevant to this study, formulating a language that breaks through and disrupts teleologically ordered discourse. This language, which in some ways is linked to the mother's body, expresses what is otherwise inexpressible. The semiotic signifies alterity; through rhythms, gaps, and a play of language the connection to the mother is recalled. The very corporeality of the language of the semiotic is juxtaposed to the abstract Law or Name which orders the symbolic, yet both are always present in the language of a socialized (non-psychotic) speaker.

The Kristevan theorization of the abject is again pertinent to my analysis. Duras presents a mother who seems to engulf her children, leaving little sense of individual personality. It would seem that without the Father's imposition of order, the process of abjection would be unending, a continual struggle for individuation against a terrifying loss of self. The "ruin and death" which is Duras' family history can therefore be seen as just this struggle to maintain or even develop "self." Some of the horror that is expressed in Duras' descriptions of this family can be located in the relation of abjection to the mother.

Orality

En effet ce dont mouraient les enfants dans la plaine

> marécageuse de Kam...c'était de la faim, des maladies de la faim et des aventures de la faim...la plaine était tellement misérable qu'elle n'avait guère d'autres richesses que ses enfants aux bouches roses toujours ouvertes sur leur faim.
>
> Un barrage contre le Pacifique

The constant refrain in *Un barrage contre le Pacifique* is that of the children of the plain dying of hunger, their pink mouths always open. Food, or the lack of food, is a central preoccupation in this text and the miserable situation of the Cambodian children is continually contrasted to the situation of Suzanne's family who eat every day.

The loss of life due to hunger is so overwhelming that the descriptions are nightmarish, giving a context for the individual tragedy of Suzanne's family, providing a background to the mother's despair that both echoes and universalizes it.

> Car il en mourait tellement que la boue de la plaine contenait bien plus d'enfants morts qu'il n'y en avait eu qui avaient eu le temps de chanter sur les buffles. Il en mourait tellement qu'on ne les pleurait plus....Il fallait bien qu'il en meure. Car si pendant quelques années seulement, les enfants de la plaine avaient cessé de mourir, la plaine en eût été à ce point infestée que sans doute, faute de pouvoir les nourrir, on les aurait donnés aux chiens, ou peut-être les aurait-on exposés aux abords de la forêt, mais même alors, qui sait, les tigres eux-mêmes auraient peut-être fini par ne plus en vouloir. (118–19)

Duras' menacing imagery of children who will either be fed or become food almost reduces natural law (represented by the tigers who do their best to help by eating all of the children that they can) to a friendly force when contrasted to man's cruelty to man. This contrast is fundamental in these texts: the dishonesty of the corrupt government agents who sell worthless land is only a part of the callous negligence of the white colonizers who close their eyes to the misery and famine that their presence has increased. This is why when the mother writes her threatening and pleading letters to the government agents she reminds them always of this greater misery and their involvement in it: "[L]es terres que vous convoitez et que vous leur enlevez, les seules terres douces de la plaine, sont grouillantes de cadavres d'enfants" (296). These crimes are interrelated: the theft of the mother's life savings and the oppression of the peasants are concretized by this image of earth that is so filled with the corpses of victims that it seems as though the cultivation of this land must use the children as fertilizer.

This catastrophe of murdered children is inseparable from the mother-child relation, as it is always, and has always been, the mothers who feed or cannot feed their children.

> Il en mourait sans doute partout....Et partout comme ici, de misère. Des mangues de la misère. Du riz de la misère. Du lait de la misère, du lait trop maigre de leurs misérables mères....Il y en avait trop et les mères les surveillaient mal. Les enfants apprenaient à marcher, à nager, à s'épouiller, à voler, à pêcher, sans la mère, mouraient sans la mère. (330–31)

In this situation, maternity is an unending torture. Women are forced to bear children that they will not be able to care for and are forced to watch them live and die in misery. Although these deaths are presented as being as constant as the rain and the sun, Duras insists on the individual sorrow: the mother who wants to look one last time at her child, the father whose duty it is, over and over again, to stamp down the mud over the grave of the child's body. This tragedy is presented as universal and eternal and yet at the same time personal and solitary.

As counterpoint to the theme of the dying children is the theme of the mother's concern with feeding her own children.

>Quand il s'agissait de les gaver, elle était toujours douce avec eux. (35)
>Les moments où ses enfants se nourrissaient trouvaient toujours la mère indulgente et patiente. (82)

These times are presented as perhaps the only moments of calm and tenderness that this family experiences. However, the word "gaver," meaning to stuff, indicates the ambivalence even in these scenes in which the mother is "douce, indulgente, patiente."

>Tu as préparé à manger. Tu m'apportes à manger. Tu me/te donnes à manger. Mais tu me/te donnes trop, comme si tu voulais me remplir tout entière avec ce que tu m'apportes. Tu te mets dans ma bouche, et j'étouffe. (*Et l'une ne bouge pas* 9)

Irigaray's text also speaks of an aggressive feeding of the child which is suffocating rather than nourishing. Thus even this primordial action which is so emphasized in the pathetic descriptions of the Cambodian women who must watch their children die from hunger can be suspect, in some way poisoned. Irigaray's imagery is of a mother filling her child with herself, endangering the child. Similarly, in *Barrage*, we see a mother who is dangerous to her children even when she is trying to care for them. Even at the end of the story, the feeding of her children still has a crucial importance for the mother. "Pendant que ses enfants mangeaient, brusquement épuisée, la mère s'assoupit. Jusque-là peut-être avait-elle douté qu'elle eût encore à le nourrir" (240).[7] It seems that when her children no longer need her to feed them (in particular her son, a point that will be developed in *L'amant*), her life will truly be over; thus in nourishing them, she is keeping herself alive.

An attention to nourishment is noticeable as well in several images that are almost surreal in contrast to the traditional realism of this novel in general. When M. Jo insinuates that his diamond ring should be returned to him Suzanne's reaction is blunt:

> Suzanne rit encore. Les millions de M. Jo n'altéraient en rien sa native innocence. Car cette bague, elle était autant à eux maintenant et aussi difficile à reprendre que s'ils l'avaient mangée, digérée, et que si elle était déjà diluée dans leur propre chair. (153)

For this family the incorporation of a diamond ring seems more easily accomplished than to nourish themselves on the "filth," storks or crocodiles, that Joseph shoots. It is also interesting that in this image the family is presented as one: the singular "leur chair" indicates a unity to this group that is only shown in the face of adversaries: M. Jo or the government agents.

In the frequent situations of family disunity, eating is often presented as difficult: the children are nauseated, particularly Suzanne, by the meat that the mother serves. When the mother is upset she does not eat and this almost seems to frighten her children. When she hides the diamond ring it is the children who have trouble eating. It is as though the family has trouble digesting its poverty. Self-hatred will not allow them to nourish themselves, almost literally closing their throats against food that others on the plain so desperately need. This is perhaps what is conveyed in the repeated image of the green mangoes that kill the peasant children every year, as they are too hungry to wait for them to ripen. The poisonous food of misery kills in many ways: by cholera caused by green mangoes or by self-starvation caused by shame.

The final mention of food in this text, following the mother's death, is perhaps the most enigmatic.

> [Suzanne] n'avait pas mangé depuis la veille mais elle était saturée d'une nourriture lourde comme du plomb et qui, semblait-il, devait lui suffire pour des jours et des jours. (360–61)

The reader is not told what this substance is but it would seem that

Suzanne has in some way ingested her mother, or perhaps her mother's life. "Tu as coulé en moi, et ce liquide chaud est devenu poison qui me paralyse" (*Et l'une ne bouge pas* 7). The image of maternal food or maternal presence which kills rather than giving life challenges the conception of our culture's most sanctified bonds. Both Duras and Irigaray are indicating that the cherished icon of mother feeding child hides a different reality. The matricide which Irigaray describes as being the foundation of our society is shown in these texts to be a daily occurrence, and one which can only victimize children as well. In a society which kills or crushes mothers, their relation to their children is both poisoned and poisonous. In *Barrage* the mother's legacy is a strange indigestible presence in Suzanne's body. Almost the only things that the mother possessed at the end of her life were her anger and her madness—perhaps these are what saturate Suzanne, what will nourish her for a long time. This final image of the daughter's incorporation of her mother suggests that although Suzanne is free to leave, she will never be free of her mother's destruction.

L'amant begins with a statement which returns to the distinction made in *Barrage* between the children of this family and the children of the plain.

> [N]ous, non, nous n'avions pas faim, nous étions des enfants blancs, nous avions honte, nous vendions nos meubles, mais nous n'avions pas faim, nous avions un boy et nous mangions, parfois, il est vrai, des saloperies, des échassiers, des petits caïmans, mais ces saloperies étaient cuites par un boy et servies par lui et parfois aussi nous les refusions, nous nous permettions ce luxe de ne pas vouloir manger. (13)

This passage contrasts the physical circumstances of the white and Asian children as well as the different sources of their suffering: instead of hunger they have shame. It is shame that they must eat, that fills their stomachs and poisons their existence. The refusal of food becomes the only defense against this shame, the only way to distinguish themselves from the peasant children. Thus denying one's hunger would be, at least partially, a revenge to take against the mother because, of course, it is the mother's fault that they are in this shameful situation. The sacred bond of nourishment between mother and child becomes the weapon to be turned against her.

The relativity of misery is also important in this passage, as it is in *Barrage*. Here it is represented by the "boy" who cooks and serves the family meals and perhaps needs this job as desperately as the corporal of *Barrage* who works without wages rather than starve. In this sense the scene of the impoverished white children refusing their food evokes a different shame that must be present when it is asked why white children do not starve to death in Indochina. The family shame becomes linked to the cultural shame of the French oppression of the people of these countries. The issue of food reminds us that this family is both oppressor and oppressed, belonging wholly to neither group.

The mad beggar woman who traverses these texts is also an expression of the terrible ambivalence of victimized maternity. She carries her baby for thousands of kilometers rather than abandon her, but refuses to take her any further, giving her at last to the mother of the narrator of *L'amant*. The question that seems to haunt each depiction of this mythic figure is whether this action of giving up her child would be called maternal sacrifice or maternal betrayal, the deepest of loves or the most callous of rejections.[8] This question is never answered.

The definition of maternal love haunts these texts as insistently as the figure of the beggar woman. While its presence is undeniable in the women of these texts, including the mother of Suzanne/the narrator of *L'amant*, its expression is sometimes contradictory. The Cambodian woman's giving up of her baby girl is perhaps comparable to the mother's frequently expressed wish for death, through which she would both abandon and free her children. The sex of the beggar woman's baby recalls that the mother-daughter bonds are *different*: one wonders if she would have abandoned a boy. The unanswered or unanswerable question of whether a mother necessarily loves her children is perhaps the mystery evoked in the passage cited at the beginning of this chapter, the mystery which will forever hold Duras before a closed door. This mystery becomes even more compelling when there is a suspicion of preference: what if a mother loves (or could love) one child and not another, perhaps a son more than a daughter? This question will be developed more clearly in *L'amant* and *L'amant de la Chine du Nord*.

Describing the beggar woman's travels across many countries the narrator says that she encounters her in Calcutta where she lives behind the French embassy. "Elle dort dans un parc, rassasiée d'une nourriture infinie" (108). This almost religious image recalls the description of Suzanne at the end of *Barrage* after her mother's death, saturated with a heavy food, but it is a more positive while equally enigmatic statement. It could be very simply that the French embassy is a good source of table scraps yet the word "infinie" suggests a less pragmatic reading. The only thing that the beggar woman seems to have infinitely is her madness. It is that, perhaps, which sates her. Thus we return to an image similar to that of the end of *Barrage*: mothers are filled with madness.[9]

Several pages before the description of the beggar woman's travels the narrator describes her terror when chased one night by this madwoman:

> Le souvenir est celui d'une peur centrale. Dire que cette peur dépasse mon entendement, ma force, c'est peu dire. Ce que l'on peut avancer, c'est le souvenir de cette certitude de l'être tout entier, à savoir que si la femme me touche, même légèrement, de la main, je passerai à mon tour dans un état bien pire que celui de la mort, l'état de la folie. (104)

Madness is easily transmissible and seems to be a particularly feminine state. Immediately following this paragraph the narrator speaks of her mother's "state" which she cannot name.

> Tard dans ma vie je suis encore dans la peur de voir s'aggraver un état de ma mère — je n'appelle pas encore cet état — ce qui la mettrait dans le cas d'être séparée de ses

enfants. Je crois que ce sera à moi de savoir ce qu'il en sera le jour venu, pas à mes frères, parce que mes frères ne sauraient pas juger cet état-là. (104)

Not only is this state transmissible between women, but it seems that only women can really evaluate it, only women really know insanity. It is perhaps a feminine mystery, like menstruation or childbirth, that cannot be easily communicated to men.

It is unclear why the mother would have to be separated from her children; the implication is that she might be dangerous to them.[10] It appears that maternal madness can turn itself against its children. This is perhaps the case with the beggar woman: her need to be unburdened becomes more important than her child. "Elle n'en veut plus du tout, elle la donne, allez, prends. Plus d'enfants. Pas d'enfant. Tous morts ou jetés, ça fait une masse à la fin de la vie" (106). When all that mothers have to feed their children is their madness, maternal love can become dangerous.

The violence that shapes this family is related to food in other ways. The narrator describes the older brother's abuse of the younger in a scene at the dinner table.

Il nous regarde manger, le petit frère et moi, et puis il pose sa fourchette, il ne regarde plus que mon petit frère. Très longuement il le regarde et puis il lui dit tout à coup, très calmement, quelque chose de terrible. La phrase est sur la nourriture. Il lui dit qu'il doit faire attention, qu'il ne doit pas manger autant....Je ne peux plus manger. Le petit frère non plus. (98–99)

There is terror in this scene which seems to refer to something unspeakable. The older brother's domination of his family is never clearly explained. The reader is told that the mother prefers him, but the narrator's insistence that this man terrorized his younger brother to death is left enigmatic. "Le frère aîné restera un assassin. Le petit frère mourra de ce frère" (72). Here the mystery of the little brother's fate is clearly connected to the absence of mother love. It would seem that the cause of his death is as much the fact of being abandoned by his mother as the malevolence of the older brother.

In this scene at the dinner table food is a pretext for bullying yet at the same time it is given an almost sacred status. To threaten someone's right to nourish himself is depicted as almost the most terrible of actions. Effectively, he prevents his siblings from eating just with his calmly stated threat. The scene has a primal quality: the older brother, by giving himself authority over the portioning out of meals, is giving himself the power of life or death over his brother. It is as though in the middle of the meal he had stated his intention to murder his brother. This is why the enraged narrator replies to him that she wishes that he were dead: it becomes more and more clear that this is a struggle to the death.

The mother's abandonment of her children to the tyranny of the oldest is presented as criminal. In a sense she sacrifices her youngest son to her oldest, just as she seems to beat her daughter for the pleasure of the beloved son.

> Je sais que le frère aîné est rivé à la porte, il écoute, il sait ce que fait ma mère, il sait que la petite est nue, et frappée, il voudrait que ça dure encore et encore jusqu'au danger. Ma mère n'ignore pas ce dessein de mon frère aîné, obscur, terrifiant. (74)

In these scenes the mother becomes the accomplice of the brother's sadism. The betrayal of the innocent children is terrible. They become victims of a mother's love, of her limitless love for her oldest son.

Although the theme of food is treated differently in *Barrage* and *L'amant*, in each case there is an important connection between a mother's ability and duty to feed her children and her insanity. In *Barrage* she seems to feed herself to her children: this "filth" represents her misery, her fury, the betrayal that she has suffered. In *L'amant* the betrayal is located in a mother's treatment of her children: their ability to be nourished is interfered with by her unpredictable violence. Because of the imbalance of what should naturally be equal, the mother's love, the children are even physically unequal: the two younger children are described as thin and weak, the older son as strong. It is as though the oldest feeds on the younger children, eventually killing his brother not only by preventing him from eating but by consuming him.

The dinner table scene is repeated in *L'amant de la Chine du Nord*, but with a crucial difference: the mother recounts the scene to her daughter, explaining that she had been listening and admitting that she had finally realized that her oldest son is dangerous. The mother's presence and remorse completely change the significance of what takes place. In *L'amant* it is a scene of violence and danger, of innocent children abandoned to a predator. In the later text, viewed through the mother's condemnation both of her son and herself, it is the beginning of the children's liberation. This is a beautiful reconciliation of mother and daughter, a redemption of maternal love.

The representation through the mother's eyes completely changes the family dynamics that have been portrayed in these texts. The mother's confession of guilt and injustice is central to this cathartic scene which is begun by a sudden surprising honesty when the daughter insists:

> — Mais pourquoi tu l'aimes comme ça et pas nous, jamais...
> La mère ment :
> — Je vous aime pareil mes trois enfants.
> L'enfant crie encore. A la faire se taire. A la gifler.
> — C'est pas vrai, pas vrai. Tu es une menteuse. Réponds pour une fois...Pourquoi tu l'aimes comme ça et pas nous?
> Silence. Et la mère répond dans un souffle :
> — Je ne sais pas pourquoi.
> Temps long. Elle ajoute :
> — Je n'ai jamais su... (25-26)

Here is a mother torn apart by a terrible problem: a preference for a dangerous, abusive child. It is as though he is her addiction. She is ashamed and acknowledges her helplessness in this terrible double abuse: she lets him hurt and terrorize the others *and* she loves him more. The girl's cry, both plea and accusation: "Pourquoi tu l'aimes comme ça et pas nous?" echoes throughout Duras' work. The absence of maternal love is tragic enough, but to see that the mother is capable of loving another mortally wounds this child. Moreover, in the case of a daughter who is continually rejected by her mother in favor of a son, the daughter's relationship to her own sex is likely to be in some way shaped by this rejection.

Similarly to the more positive representation of the mother in this last text, the beggar woman who was another symbol of maternal madness is also presented with more sympathy. When the child talks to her lover about the beggar women she explains, "Qu'elles n'ont plus aucune raison, toutes folles à force d'avoir eu peur, à force de leurs enfants morts de faim..." (107). In this description the women are driven mad by maternal love, by their helplessness to save their children, perhaps by the responsibility in which they have failed as supposed sources of nourishment and life. Each story, that of the family and that of the women of French Indochina, shows women as victims in various ways of society and madness. The destruction of the mothers in these texts is shown to be universal, transcending cultural and historical categorizations, transmitted from one generation to another.

In the passage quoted above the child also explains why the beggar women are so frightening, "Ce sont ces femmes qui font le plus peur. Parce qu'elles rient en même temps qu'elles pleurent" (107). Here it is not the fear of contagion which frightens the child, but it is a breaking down of boundaries between laughter and tears, rejoicing and grieving. In the same way that their emotions are bursting forth uncontrolled, the women themselves are not contained by any frontier: they wander over the mountains and through the forests—talking, screaming, singing, laughing, and crying.

In a way the beggar women resemble the lepers who are also omnipresent in these texts. Lepers wander, are mad and frightening, and their laughter is often mentioned as part of the background of the sounds of these countries. In Duras' writings on this society, the smell of leprosy is as constant as the sight of dying children or the sound of the laughter of the mad mothers. These tragic victims of society's callous rejection are presented as the human base on which this culture is built. Their rotting flesh (whether destroyed by leprosy, maggots, or cholera) is as necessary to the colonizers as food. They are the sustenance of the colonies.

Thus the madness of mothers is continually represented as a personal and a social tragedy, each image reflecting the other. The concern with food is used to signal their responsibility and their terrible helplessness in the face of so much injustice and oppression. Both victims and victimizers, mothers often balance on the frontiers between lucidity and delirium, apathy and destructiveness.

Both the unease evoked by a lack of distinction between categories and the theme of orality recall Julia Kristeva's formulation of the abject. The process of abjection occurs in the chaos of the original mother-infant dyad. At this point in the child's development much of her existence is subsumed in the act of feeding. The mother's availability to the child thus dominates the child's pre-conscious. Although the child does not conceive of the mother as separate, her hunger and its satisfaction are her connection to her surroundings. Due to this focus on orality, any pre-conscious phantasies of mother-infant interaction would involve imagery of both engulfment and introjection. This oral phase could be a time of intense emotion for the infant who might feel fear and rage, frustration and loss as well as pleasure and contentment derived from satisfaction of needs and wants.

The intense emotion that would accompany this need of the mother is present in some of the scenes that I have examined in Duras' texts. The mother is sometimes portrayed as very powerful and frightening; the disappointment and rage associated with what is seen as betrayal or insufficient care are overwhelming. This mother (generalized by her lack of a name so that she often seems to have the status of a universalized "Mother") is depicted as a force of nature: terrible, destructive, unpredictable, pitiless.

[Suzanne] en oubliait que cette force venait de sa mère et la subissait comme elle aurait subi celle du vent, des vagues, une force impersonnelle. (*Barrage* 137)

Like the sea (*mer*), the mother (*mère*) is an overwhelming force that can almost obliterate her daughter. (The daughter's "saturation" at her mother's death suggests that her mother invades and takes over her very cells.) This is exactly what the infant tries to defend herself against through abjection. The fear is of being swallowed, surrounded, perhaps permeated by the other. Kristeva uses the image of the skin that forms on warm milk to exemplify the nauseating in between state of the abject. This viscous skin is not only in between, semi-solid/semi-liquid, it also evokes the first nourishment ever received.

> Le dégoût alimentaire est peut-être la forme la plus élémentaire et la plus archaïque de l'abjection...Avec le vertige qui brouille le regard, la *nausée* me cambre, contre cette crème de lait, et me sépare de la mère, du père qui me la présentent. (*Pouvoirs de l'horreur* 10)

Both the "filth" that the family is forced to eat and their frequent reluctance to eat can be related not only to their poverty and their shame, but also to the ambiguity of the mother's role in feeding her children. The fear that the children have concerning their mother and what she feeds them is similar to the repulsion that Kristeva describes as part of abjection.

The transgression of different states which is part of abjection is frequently found in the references to the beggar women, not only in the laughter and crying previously noted, but also in the repeated mentions of the putrefying flesh of the beggar woman's foot. Not only is this foot horrifyingly poised between solid and liquid, it is also transgressing another boundary by its status of food to the maggots that infest it. Maggots are more generally known to feed on corpses; thus the beggar woman is presented as in between life and death, another manifestation of the horrifying non-state of abjection. There are repeated references in these texts to the potential status of people (particularly children) as food. Not only are children eaten by tigers, they are devoured from the inside by worms (which is what happens to the baby that the beggar woman abandons). The fears are multiple: there is a fear of being engulfed, there is also a fear of being attacked from the inside.

The uncertainty of the status of children in these texts, eating or being eaten, attacked from within and without, illustrates the unspeakable terror of the abject and foregrounds the mother-child relation which is its origin. The devouring mother, this monstrous *mer/mère*, seems to be a particular danger for the daughter. Whether she overwhelms her will and drowns her individuality, or feeds her her own insanity and saturates her with this loss of self, the menace to the daughter is the basis of the abject terror that is present in each of the versions of this story that Duras tells.

Kristeva posits that it is the intervention of the third party which helps to bring about an end to this symbiosis which is both idyllic and nightmarish. The infant's recognition of the mother's desire for another would possibly help to stabilize boundaries for this fragile pre-ego. In this sense it is possible that it is the absence of the father in these texts which maintains the abjection implicit in Duras' representation. As there is no paternal intervention, there is no protection or diversion from the mother's overwhelming force. The missing Law of the Father is thus responsible for the near psychosis presented as existing in the mother-daughter relation. It is not until the daughter develops her own sexuality and herself brings a man into the relation that she seems to be freed somewhat of her mother's power. Until another phallic intervention can assist the daughter's entry into the symbolic order, she floats in a semiotic confusion of identity.

The titles of these texts could be suggestive of this struggle. *Un barrage contre le Pacifique* would suggest the hopelessness of trying to hold back the *mer/mère* whose dominance is presented as inevitable in the earlier texts. *L'Eden Cinéma* could be said to evoke the idyllic aspect of the mother-child dyad. *L'amant* would be the barrier that the daughter finally succeeds in imposing between the mother and herself, her own desire for another freeing her from this poisonous relation.

The lack of boundaries between mother and daughter might also explain the frightening shift that the narrator of *L'amant* experiences in her view of her mother, just before leaving for France at the age of eighteen.

> J'ai regardé ma mère. Je l'ai mal reconnue. Et puis, dans une sorte d'effacement soudain, de chute, brutalement je ne l'ai plus reconnue du tout. Il y a eu tout à coup, là, près de moi, une personne assise à la place de ma mère, elle n'était pas ma mère, elle avait son aspect, mais jamais elle n'avait été ma mère....L'épouvante ne tenait pas à ce que je dis d'elle, de ses traits, de son air de bonheur, de sa beauté, elle venait de ce qu'elle était assise là même où était assise ma mère lorsque la substitution s'était produite, que je savais que personne d'autre n'était là à sa place qu'elle-même, mais que justement cette identité qui n'était remplaçable par aucune autre avait disparu et que j'étais sans aucun moyen de faire qu'elle revienne, qu'elle commence à revenir. *Rien ne se proposait plus pour habiter l'image.* Je suis devenue folle en pleine raison. (105–06 my emphasis)

There are many possible readings of this ambiguous passage, but I would suggest that it is the frightening insubstantiality of the mother's individuality that inspires such horror in the daughter. It is as though the image is supposed to contain this fluid thing, the identity, but has failed to do so. In the same way that the narrator relies on an image at the beginning of this text to "characterize" her young self (I will return to this point in the next section), she had relied on the image of her mother, which seems suddenly invaded by an other. The (m)other that is described in this passage seems to eject the daughter from the symbolic order of "pleine raison" into the psychosis which is immersion in the semiotic. The daughter's situating of her identity is so dependent on her mother's that she is "othered" from her self.

The suggestions of substitution, replacement, or possession by

Orality and Specularity

another recall the fear of contagion or invasion described as part of abjection. Perhaps if the mother can be so easily possessed, the daughter will suffer the same fate. Indeed, the word "possession" with its connotation not only of invasion by another identity, but also of madness, reminds us of the narrator's terror of the contagion of her mother's insanity. This transmission seems to have taken place at the end of this passage. Engulfed by her mother's madness, the daughter is doomed. Madness becomes her identity.

Specularity

> Et n'ayant jamais connu ton visage, ne m'avais-tu nourrie d'inanition?

> *Et l'une ne bouge pas sans l'autre*

Specularity is the basis of the relationship between Suzanne and M. Jo in *Un barrage contre le Pacifique*; it is founded on his payments to her for allowing him to look at her.[11] Interestingly, it is he who establishes this relation. When Suzanne is about to let him see her nude, he promises her a new phonograph, reducing this interaction to a commercial exchange. "C'est ainsi qu'au moment où elle alla ouvrir et se donner à voir au monde, le monde la prostitua" (73). Suzanne's desire is passive. She wants to be the object of M. Jo's look and that seems to be all that she wants. M. Jo, however, requires that there be an exchange that assures Suzanne's status as object. This begins to change Suzanne's vision of herself.

> Parfois les mains de M. Jo rencontraient les seins de Suzanne.
> Et une fois, il dit :
> — Tu as de beaux seins....
> Et au-dessus de la ville terrifiante, Suzanne vit ses seins, elle vit l'érection de ses seins plus haut que tout ce qui se dressait dans la ville dont c'était eux qui auraient raison....Il la regardait de très près. Elle, en regardant la ville ne regardait

qu'elle-même. Regardait solitairement son empire, où régneraient ses seins, sa taille, ses jambes. (226–27)

The dismemberment of this body that would rule over the city has been carried out by the look of M. Jo. His objectification has, in a sense, mutilated Suzanne's relationship to her body, separating not only various body parts from each other but also separating Suzanne from her body, so that she can see it towering over the city. Suzanne has begun to see herself through the eyes of an other.

As Suzanne's identity becomes more and more transformed by this mediation of her self-image, the cinema is given a larger role in this story. In the second part of *Barrage* the family is in a large city trying to sell the diamond ring. Joseph abandons his mother and sister so that he can pursue women. Suzanne, however, spends her days in the darkness of the theatre, living a romantic dream.

Il dit je vous aime. Elle dit je vous aime moi aussi. Le ciel sombre de l'attente s'éclaire d'un coup. Foudre d'un tel baiser. Gigantesque communion de la salle et de l'écran. On voudrait bien être à leur place. Ah! comme on le voudrait. Leurs corps s'enlacent. Leurs bouches s'approchent, avec la lenteur du cauchemar. Une fois qu'elles sont proches à se toucher, on les mutile de leurs corps. Alors, dans leurs têtes de décapités, on voit ce qu'on ne saurait voir, leurs lèvres les unes en face des autres s'entrouvrir, s'entrouvrir encore, leurs mâchoires se défaire comme dans la mort.... (189)

This grotesque fragmentation of bodies prefigures Suzanne's vision of her own breasts triumphing over the city; the two passages are very similar in their monstrous exaggeration of the human body, mixing passion and death, sex and mutilation. It would seem that cinematic specularity continues the work on Suzanne's psyche that M. Jo began. In the theatre Suzanne becomes even more alienated from her body, her self, her own desires so that her perceptions of these are entirely mediated by others, real or fictional. Her sexuality has become specularized. "C'était là seulement, devant l'écran que ça devenait simple. D'être ensemble avec un inconnu devant une même image, vous donnait l'envie de l'inconnu" (223). It is the shared image, the same view, which is important for Suzanne. Similarly, when she sees herself, her own body, she needs to participate in the view that the other has of this body.

The importance of specula(riza)tion, therefore, is not only the image that the woman gives to the man, but the image of self that is given to her. The presentation of self-view in these texts recalls Jacques Lacan's "Le stade du miroir comme formateur de la fonction du je," where the image of self which is reflected from a mirror or another person's face forms (illusorily) one's self-image. Lacan explains that the reflected image contradicts the previous impression of a "corps morcelé," or body in pieces. In this text it is the opposite. Suzanne's mediated self-view is of a body in pieces, yet this does not frighten her; rather, she finds a justification for this view in front of movie screens. This image of bodies dismembered by a gaze is equivocal: it is inherently violent yet normalized by the process to which Suzanne is submitted. To continue the comparison to Lacan's mirror phase, it would seem that it was not possible for Suzanne to receive an affirming reflection of herself from her mother, who is too lost in her madness to give this recognition. "A chacune, sa représentation fait défaut. Son visage, l'animation de son corps manque" (*Et l'une ne bouge pas* 20). Suzanne is reduced to taking on an image which fragments rather than unifies her. Thus the Imaginary within which she has found her first understanding of self and other is an Imaginary which is both cinematized and misogynized, a specular economy in which her place is only assured by what she has to show.

In *L'amant* the image of self is dominant from the first page.[12] The narrator introduces the events that she will recount with reference to several self-images; more precisely, she contrasts the view of her *face* at the time of the writing of this text to an *image* of her younger self. The narration shifts confusingly between these two—the destruction of the face and the preservation of the image.

It is through the image that the narrator recognizes herself.

> Je pense souvent à cette image que je suis seule à voir encore et dont je n'ai jamais parlé...C'est entre toutes celle qui me plaît de moi-même, celle où je me reconnais, où je m'enchante. (9)

However, she contrasts the fact that there has never been a photograph of this image that only she can see, to the actuality of the face, and gives predominance to the not-seen, the nonexistent. "C'est à ce manque d'avoir été faite qu'elle doit sa vertu, celle de représenter un absolu, d'en être justement l'auteur" (17). An absolute is commonly defined as: "Ce qui existe indépendamment de toute condition ou de tout rapport avec autre chose" (*Petit Robert* 8), that which exists without any reference or relation to anything else. This would seem to be in complete opposition to the way in which we define language. In this text, memory is more important (or perhaps more reliable) than language, the image has predominance over the face in that this image is in some way outside of signification whereas the face which is being discussed tells a story of devastation. "[J]'ai vu s'opérer ce vieillissement de mon visage avec l'intérêt que j'aurais pris par exemple au déroulement d'une lecture" (10).

The abrupt shifts between discussions of face and image are only one of the many ways in which this text is destabilized from the very beginning. The insistence on the visual disrupts the authority of *écriture*. This text is always about representation in various forms and the insistence on the image reminds the reader that both language and vision rely on the ability to fix or freeze something which is always in movement.

> L'histoire de ma vie n'existe pas. Ça n'existe pas. Il n'y a jamais de centre. Pas de chemin, pas de ligne. Il y avait de vastes endroits où l'on fait croire qu'il y avait quelqu'un, ce n'est pas vrai il n'y avait personne. (14)[13]

Again in this passage the reader is presented with nonexistence as something that is significative. Duras' "autobiography" can be seen as layers of representation: her writing represents an image which itself represents her creation of her self.

The explanation of the choice to wear a man's hat is pertinent to this analysis of self-representation:

> Soudain je me vois comme une autre, comme une autre serait vue, au-dehors, mise à la disposition de tous, mise à la disposition de tous les regards, mise dans la circulation des villes, des routes, du désir. (20)

The hat helps the narrator to achieve a different mirroring, it brings about a rupture of the usual self-seeing-self and changes it to self-seeing-other/self, which is a dissection of "identity." Her objectification of her self through her own gaze makes her available to all. Any gaze can transform her to anything: "Ce que je veux paraître je le parais...tout ce que l'on veut de moi je peux le devenir" (26). Image dictates being. Both of these passages speak also of the desire of the other: availability to the gaze is equated to submission to the other's desire.

The chain of references in these pages, image-representation-desire-loss of identity, not only problematizes the author/narrator/character relationship that is so central to the notion of autobiography, it also relates this text to *Barrage*. There is a link between the emphasis on cinema and cinematic vision at the end of *Barrage* and the extremely cinematic presentation of the story in *L'amant*. Although many of Duras' works could be described as merging to some extent the categories of novel and screenplay, in this text this technique is inextricable from the story that is recounted. This is the story of a young woman and how she is created by the gaze.[14]

Irigaray's description of woman's reduction to a mirror reflecting what man needs to see is very pertinent to both of these texts. The texts seem to suggest that the way that women are looked at and the way that they look at themselves is different from a man's experience as the object of the gaze, either someone else's or his own. In *Barrage* Suzanne's semi-prostitution suggests the objectified relation of women to their own bodies; in *L'amant* it is more directly addressed. The narrator describes the lives of the white women who live in the colonies:

> Il y en a de très belles, de très blanches, elles prennent un soin extrême de leur beauté ici, surtout dans les postes de brousse. Elles ne font rien, elles se gardent seulement....Elles attendent. Elles s'habillent pour rien. Elles se regardent. (27)

The specificity of the woman's role in the specular economy of Western culture is important in these texts. Without women's complicity, this aspect of male dominance could not function. Women need to see themselves as objects to help men to see them as objects. The two similar phrases in the passage quoted above: "Elles se gardent" and "Elles se regardent," emphasize this link between objectification and specula(riza)tion.

The choice of a woman's representation of herself (insofar as she has a choice) comes to seem almost the most important choice of her life. The white women of the colonies are doomed to sterile and futile attempts to preserve their looks; the narrator frees herself from her family by advertising her availability. The descriptions of Hélène Lagonelle insist on her lack of self-representation: "Seule Hélène Lagonelle échappait à la loi de l'erreur. Attardée dans l'enfance" (28). The "error" refers back to the description of the women of the colonies who spend their lives on their appearance: "Ce manquement des femmes à elles-mêmes par elles-mêmes opéré m'apparaissait toujours comme une erreur" (28). In other words, women are missing to themselves or abstract themselves in order to please men. Hélène's inability to perform this self-mutilation, to see herself as women are seen by men, is fortunate in that she will not waste herself on what could be called a masquerade of femininity. Her identity is only based on her own view of herself unmediated by any other. Yet she is presented as both lucky and lacking; her freedom from male specula(riza)tion leaves her outside the sexual economy and prevents her from participating in her society.

The only woman whose self-representation is not discussed is the mother. The impression given is that instead of representing a self to others, she represents nothing. However, this lack which in Hélène Lagonelle derives from a strange innocence, is in this case due to loss of self; she does not even have the appearance of self that most women have. It is as though to look in her eyes is to see only emptiness and devastation, a frightening void. Since it is the possibility of being engulfed in this void which terrifies the daughter, this could also explain the daughter's insistence on her own self-representation. The more that she is seen by others (therefore validated by their gaze), the less she is in danger of taking on her mother's loss.

> Avec ton lait, ma mère, tu m'as donné la glace. Et, si je pars, tu perds l'image de la vie, de ta vie. Et si je demeure, ne suis-je le dépôt de ta mort? (*Et l'une ne bouge pas* 20)

In Irigaray's representation of the dangers of this relationship the mother feeds her child her own lack of self. The word "glace" can be read as meaning either ice or mirror but in this context I would suggest that the emphasis is on the mirror that the mother gives to her child so that the child can reflect an image back to her mother. This is again an inversion of Lacan's theorization of the mirror phase as Irigaray makes the mother dependent on her daughter for a coherent self-view. The daughter's responsibility to the mother is given predominance, but is also shown to be an impossible choice between murder and suicide. If she leaves her mother she takes her mother's life with her, yet if she stays she must be permeated with her death. Irigaray's description expresses precisely the dilemma that holds Suzanne in *Barrage*—in the end she risks her own destruction. The reversed mother-daughter mirroring in which the daughter must reflect her mother becomes a *mise en abîme* which the daughter must shatter to save herself.

In *L'amant* the lover's gaze is presented as a way out of this inherited loss of self. Not only does this gaze establish an image of the girl which is opposed to her mother's empty gaze, but it redefines corporeality.

> Il la regarde. Les yeux fermés il la regarde encore...Il discerne de moins en moins clairement les limites de ce corps, celui-ci n'est pas comme les autres, il n'est pas fini, dans la chambre il grandit encore, il est encore sans formes arrêtées, à tout instant en train de se faire, il n'est pas seulement là où il le voit, il est ailleurs aussi, il s'étend au-delà de la vue, vers le jeu, la mort.... (121)

In this passage the emphasis is not only on the fact that it is an adolescent's body and thus still developing, it is also on the body as the force which dominates this story. In general, the body, like the face, is not always representational. Yet in this text both are significative. Specula(riza)tion dismembers women, separating them from their bodies and separating body parts from each other. This body in pieces signifies (among other things) the mastery of the male in the sexual economy of our culture. Therefore, although bodies are not inherently representational, an aspect of specula(riza)tion is to insert the female body into the symbolic order signifying the status of woman as other and the accrual of phallic power to the man.

The lover's gaze also challenges the family's refusal of interaction:

Non seulement on ne se parle pas mais on ne se regarde pas. Du moment qu'on est vu, on ne peut pas regarder. Regarder c'est avoir un mouvement de curiosité vers, envers, c'est déchoir. Aucune personne regardée ne vaut le regard sur elle. Il est toujours déshonorant. (69)

To look is to desire and desire demeans its subject. While the lover's existence is taken up by desire, the family of the narrator seems to expend all of its energy in repression. The chain of associations that was located in the first pages: image-representation-desire-loss of identity is here transformed to look-desire-loss. In the first case it is a question of being looked at, in the second, looking. In this dysfunctional family it is more threatening to be in the subject position (of the gaze, of desire) than in the object position. The word "déchoir," meaning to fall to an inferior position, emphasizes the struggle within this family, and which it projects outside itself, to have power over others. However, this power is sometimes arrived at through denial of self, especially for the young woman.

Corresponding to this insistence on being the object rather than the subject of the gaze, there is throughout this text an emphasis on the narrator's passivity. Even the phrasing of the condemnations of her actions that she repeats, "[C]ette petite vicieuse va se faire caresser le corps par un sale Chinois millionnaire" (109–10), "[E]lle va se faire découvrir le corps par le milliardaire chinois" (112), emphasizes her body as the recipient of the actions and desires of her lover. It is as though her only possibility of existence in her family and her society is to make herself available to others' desires. In this way her own desire is occulted or at least mystified; the reader is told of the narrator's pleasure, yet more as an object of desire than as subject.[15]

> Il la prend comme il prendrait son enfant. Il prendrait son enfant de même. Il joue avec le corps de son enfant, il le retourne, il s'en recouvre le visage, la bouche, les yeux. Et elle, elle continue à s'abandonner dans la direction exacte qu'il a prise quand il a commencé à jouer. (123)

Here the narrator becomes the child or even the toy of the lover. She is completely passive, to the point of letting him cover her eyes, emphasizing the fact that she can only be the object of the gaze.

This extreme passivity is a part of the play of specula(riza)tion in this text. The narrator's pleasure seems to be found only in her objectification: through the gaze or in the sexual act. The unstable notion of self that was noted earlier is resolved by the transformation of self into thing. The narrator's identity is only affirmed when she is an object to others. This is complicated by the fact that in prostituting herself she is both defying and complying with the mother's wishes. What the mother wants of her daughter is contradictory: she wants her to be respectable and virginal yet she wants her to get money for the family in whatever manner is necessary.

> Reste cette petite-là qui grandit et qui, elle, saura peut-être un jour comment on fait venir l'argent dans cette maison. C'est pour cette raison, elle ne le sait pas, que la mère permet à son enfant de sortir dans cette tenue d'enfant prostituée. (33)

Perhaps the only way in which the daughter can obey her mother's contradictory demands is precisely in the objectification that she practices on herself.

In these four texts, the mother's role in her daughter's self-representation seems to work at both a psychoanalytic and a socioeconomic level. I have discussed how the lack of an affirming gaze from a mother who cannot establish her own self-view must damage the daughter's ability to represent her self. It is also important to note that the mother's marketing of her daughter is a transmission of the male view of woman as object, mutating the daughter's self-image in a different way. Both of these failures in the daughter's self-view place the final responsibility on her, rather than on her mother. In the failure of the mirror phase she must find a way to view herself and to reflect a view back to the mother. In her participation in specula(riza)tion she is required to establish her place as sexualized merchandise. The alliance of maternal and masculine needs involves a deformation of self founded on acceptance of objectification and passivity. The negation of the mother in our culture actually impels the daughter toward the phallic gaze, searching for a refuge from the mother's non-existence.

The intertwined themes of specula(riza)tion, passivity, and objectification are continued in *L'amant de la Chine du Nord*. Indeed, the repetition of "Il la regarde" and variations of this phrase is almost overwhelming. This insistent vision of desire is articulated by Duras in one of her notes:

> En cas de film tout se passerait ainsi par le regard. L'enchaînement ce serait le regard. Ceux qui regardent sont regardés à leur tour par d'autres. La caméra annule la réciprocité : elle ne filme que les gens, c'est-à-dire la solitude de chacun...C'est des gens seuls, des "solitudes" de hasard. La passion est l'enchaînement du film. (166)

In this note, passion and the gaze are conflated and they are the metonymic chain which gives the film meaning. This diacritical movement separates the characters; there is no reciprocity of look, or of desire. While in *L'amant* the conflation of looking and desiring was degrading to the subject, here there is no shame, but it is not made clear whether looking/desiring increases the solitude of each character, or simply cannot change it.

Similarly, in another important note, Duras insists on the view of the girl: "Une sorte de Miss France-enfant ferait s'effondrer le film tout entier. Plus encore : elle le ferait disparaître. La beauté ne fait rien. Elle ne regarde pas. Elle est regardée" (70). The girl must act as a magnet for the gaze of the spectator (both the lover and the viewer of the film), yet it is the gaze rather than the object of the gaze which is central. Once again, this note emphasizes the lack of reciprocity. The subject and object of the gaze cannot be the same.

It would seem that at the end of the text, there is reciprocity of view for the first time; yet this comes after physical separation. When the lover comes to see the departure of the boat that is taking the girl to France, for a moment "Ils ne se regardent pas. Se voient" (215). Here the lovers *see* each other, almost involuntarily, rather than *looking* at each other. Even this however seems to confer too much equality: the girl closes her eyes, relinquishing the possibility of a subject position in the specular economy. The final image of the two is the lover looking at the girl who has her eyes closed. Once again she is only the object of his gaze.

The text of *L'amant de la Chine du Nord* does not address the specularization of women as pointedly as *L'amant*. One of the many elements which contrast this text to the earlier one is an insistence on the particularity of this relationship: the lovers are presented much more as individuals than in *L'amant*, where there was more of a focus on the connections to family, to community, to culture. In this sense it would seem that there is a decreasing attention to social problems from *Barrage* to *L'amant*, and then to *L'amant de la Chine du Nord*; the last of these texts seems pared down to the fewest possible elements. It seems that the entire visual focus of this text is the lover looking at the child (and the camera looking at the couple). The essence of this relationship and of this story is desire and love. Money is not as important as in the earlier texts, nor is the colonial society in which the lovers live. While the family of the girl still plays a prominent role, it seems to exercise less power over her; there is not the same sense of foreboding, of horror and evil as in *L'amant*. This is a love story.

> Le Chinois la regarde à bout de bras pour mieux la voir.
> Il la regarde "pour toujours en une fois" avant la fin de l'histoire d'amour. (192)

These three texts could be described as tragedies: *Barrage* a social tragedy, *L'amant* a family tragedy, and *L'amant de la Chine du Nord* a personal tragedy. Despite its very modern form, the content of this latest text could be seen as an almost classical story of two lovers doomed by differences of family and culture to live apart.

As in *L'amant* the objectification of the girl is clearly enunciated:

> Elle devient objet à lui, à lui seul secrètement prostituée. Sans plus de nom. Livrée comme une chose, chose pour lui seul, volée. Par lui seul prise, utilisée, pénétrée. Chose tout à coup inconnue, une enfant sans autre identité que celle de lui appartenir à lui, d'être à lui seul son bien, sans mot pour nommer ça, fondue à lui, diluée dans une généralité pareillement naissante, celle depuis le commencement des temps nommée à tort par un autre mot, celui d'indignité. (96)

Even more explicitly than in the passage quoted from *L'amant* in which the lover uses and plays with the girl almost as a doll, here she becomes not only a thing but his thing. There are several points to be noted in this important passage. The first is the notion of finance that is conveyed by the words "prostituée, livrée, volée." The lover's sexual possession of the girl is inseparable from their economic situations. However, the final line of the passage would seem to deny the common understanding of this transaction by correcting the word "shamefulness" (*indignité*) that might be used as a label. The refutation of socially imposed values and standards and the refusal of shame or degradation is a central theme of all three of the texts, although less explicitly in *Barrage*. The choice that the girl makes to objectify herself seems to invert most common categorizations or definitions: of shamefulness, of pleasure, of love.

There is also an emphasis on loss of identity in the passage above. The girl loses her name, becomes unknown, loses all identity except as a possession. In both *L'amant* and *L'amant de la Chine du Nord* there is an emphasis on anonymity, specifically on the interchangeability of women as sexual objects, but this is presented positively. The loss of identity that was noted at the beginning of *L'amant* as produced by the gaze, is here produced through the sexual act. Yet in each case this is the girl's desire. This non-identity which is so terrifying when faced with the mother's needs is looked for in the sexual relation. Words evoking liquidity emphasize this merging: "fondue" and "diluée" recall Suzanne's "saturation" in *Barrage*, but here the girl is looking for annihilation. In this manner she loses her identity but is reborn as object, as possession.

Woman as object to be seen, taken, stolen, and sold is central both to the girl's relationship with her lover and with her family. It is perhaps the interconnection which helps to give this story its complexity, for the love story cannot be untouched by the family history and the familial relationships seem to predestine this affair with the Chinese man. The narrowing focus that was noted: *Barrage*—society, *L'amant*—family, *L'amant de la Chine du Nord*

—lovers, does not completely exclude the other levels of self in relation to others. In these texts they are always interrelated.

The status of women in the sexual economy—in the structuring of our sexuality and in the commerce of sexuality—traverses all of these levels. The family's attitude toward the girl as merchandise reflects social standards which are also accepted, at least partially, by the lover. When talking to her about her family's situation he is blunt: "C'est vrai que vous n'avez plus rien. La seule chose qui leur restait à vendre c'était toi. Et on ne veut pas t'acheter" (146). The presentation of colonial society normalizes the family's prostitution of the girl, just as the sorrow and insanity of the family normalize the girl's behavior with the man. All of these relationships are intertwined and the link between them is an economic one. Even in *L'amant de la Chine du Nord*, where the relationship between the girl and her lover is portrayed as a love affair, money cannot be ignored. The girl knows that her desire for this man is inseparable from his wealth.

Luce Irigaray's situating of specula(riza)tion as one of the more important tactics of male domination deepens an understanding of the interweaving of the themes of the gaze and of money in Duras' texts. In each case it is the man (or men) who has both the financial power and the power of the gaze. It is men who impose on one hand starvation, misery, and death through unjust economic practices and on the other hand insanity and alienation from self through specular domination. For one of the most horrible forms of oppression that Duras depicts in these "biomythographies" is the loss of self which can accompany the physical misery of oppression. In the case of the beggar women who wander Indochina laughing and crying, in the case of the mother who is slowly emptied out by her rage and despair, one could say that they no longer recognize themselves and that this is the most tragic aspect of their defeat.

The position of Suzanne/the narrator/the girl in these stories is different from that of the other women in these texts in that she seems to recognize and choose this loss of self through specula(riza)tion and through this she is not destroyed, only mutated. It is perhaps this mutation which shows itself in her face as a bizarre and premature aging. It is possible that by choosing the total objectification that was described in *L'amant de la Chine du Nord*, where not only is she endlessly looked at but she is presented as a purchase, she can emerge on the other side of the mirror to a different possibility of self-view and self-representation. It is this mutation which makes these texts so difficult to discuss as autobiography, in that the self-representation that one might expect to find in a text described as autobiographical is layered and inverted in these variations on a central story. These texts represent a self at the moment of its loss of self-representation. They recount the impossibility (or the falsity) of their own project.

The specula(riza)tion of this character thus, in its exposure of different types of masculine power, destabilizes the concept of identity which is the basis of autobiography. The reader, in being so specifically directed to look at the girl (particularly in the two later texts), is caught up in the examination of specular power and finds herself seemingly participating in the oppression of women by men, children by parents, Asians by whites. This divided positioning of the reader (divided in the sense that the content encourages abhorrence of these oppressions while the form insinuates complicity) is linked to the ambivalence of the position of the girl who is a child, a woman, poor, yet white. The position of the Chinese man is correspondingly problematized: he is an adult, a man, rich, yet Asian.[16]

A divided vision splits these texts; nothing is unequivocal. The fluctuations of power, identity, and desire undermine any one reading of these stories. The narrator's description of her prostitution is an example of this fragmented view. By submerging herself willingly and totally in "shame," she destabilizes the common understanding of her position, so that it is presented as both terrible and wonderful. Her portrayal of her mother is another case of divided emotions and views. "[J]e crois avoir dit l'amour que l'on portait à notre mère mais je ne sais pas si j'ai dit la haine qu'on lui portait aussi ..." (*L'amant* 34). While she understands the tragedy of her mother's life, she cannot forgive the fact that the victimization was transmitted to the children.

The murdered mother

La vie était terrible et la mère était aussi terrible que la vie.

Un barrage contre le Pacifique

The mother-daughter relationship represented in these texts is a relationship of extremes: hate and adoration, terror and guilt are intermingled. The dual role of the mother as victim of society and of men but also victimizer of her daughter splits the view of this figure. This story, told again and again, does not so much attempt to resolve these oppositions as to speak them, as though speech in itself could free the narrator from the closed door outside which she still waits. She is still the child alone in front of a frightening mystery which could be understood as the unspeakable mystery of her mother's rejection of her youngest children in favor of her oldest son.

The motifs of orality and specularity help to elucidate the complexity of the mother-daughter relation. The emphasis on eating, particularly the instability of children's position (whether they will eat or be eaten), confronts the reader with the grief of mother-child relations which fail at the most basic level. The images of engulfment, contamination, and rot demonstrate the primal fear of devourment. By means of this motif Duras returns the "civilization" that she portrays to the level of the law of the jungle. One is predator or preyed upon. The savagery of the life in French Indochina is perhaps most dominant in *Barrage*, where it seems that death and putrefaction are omnipresent. In *L'amant* the concern with eating is linked to violence and insanity: the rot is in the family itself.

Nous sommes ensemble dans une honte de principe d'avoir à vivre la vie. C'est là que nous sommes au plus profond de

> notre histoire commune, celle d'être tous les trois des enfants de cette personne de bonne foi, notre mère, que la société a assassinée. Nous sommes du côté de cette société qui a réduit ma mère au désespoir. A cause de ce qu'on a fait à notre mère si aimable, si confiante, nous haïssons la vie, nous nous haïssons. (*L'amant* 69)

The murder of the mother poisons the children's existence. Her despair contaminates her children so that they turn against themselves. Yet it would seem that even this shared desolation is convoluted in that the children's self-hatred comes from their self-blame. Feeling themselves to be allies with the persecutors of their mother, the children can only turn their grief and fear inwards. They are devoured internally by the mother's legacy.

In *L'amant de la Chine du Nord*, perhaps the least tragic of these texts, orality has a less important place, the terrors that it evokes are somewhat removed; the beggar woman, the violence of the older brother are not as threatening. The motif of orality emphasizes the links between people: whether mother and child, or members of a community, interdependence is necessary for survival. However, interdependence is only partially functional in these texts: mothers cannot always feed their children or sometimes they poison them with their own helpless violence. Society allows some of its members to take the food of others. The social contract is often oppression; the familial bond is occasionally insanity. The image of shared food in these texts often expresses devastation rather than community.

The motif of specularity also reveals betrayals within both familial and societal groups. The possibility of self-representation is shown to vary depending on the power of the person who is seeking to establish an identity. The girl's image is dictated by her mother, her society, and her lover. Her only power is to choose consciously to abdicate identity, a contradiction that perhaps saves a shred of sanity. This inversion of empowerment, the sacrifice of her ability to name herself, is in many ways dictated by her fear of her mother, of either her brutality or her defeat. She chooses sexual annihilation rather than eradication within her family. In *Barrage* Suzanne's contamination by an objectifying gaze shows the mutilation of women in the specular economy. In *L'amant* the "image" of the narrator is important yet problematized: this text is also an investigation of the mechanisms of self-representation. In *L'amant de la Chine du Nord* it is the lover's gaze which predominates and the girl is reduced to what others want of her: object, toy, whore, thing.

The cinematic style of the two later texts brings the reader into the play of specula(riza)tion: it becomes more and more evident that everyone is involved in the subjection of others to the gaze (although some more than others). Both the girl's and the reader's complicity are disturbing elements of these stories. Victim and victimizer are not always clearly distinguished in this relation, or perhaps it could be said that in specula(riza)tion there is never total power matched by total lack. There is some power, although it is a different power, in both the subject and the object positions.

Each of the texts that I have discussed tells the reader something new or different about the mother-daughter relation yet there is the impression that there will always be more to tell, that this tale is endless. The link between the mother's and daughter's destinies is also presented as unending: everything that the daughter lives in her lifetime must be in some way connected to the destruction of her mother. This is, perhaps, the central image of this story: the two lives intertwined like the jungle vines to which Duras frequently refers in her descriptions of the setting of her childhood, vines which strangle, yet are separable only through violence and destruction. It is the presentation of this family in its social context which shows the mother as both all-powerful and powerless, and thus relates this personal tragedy to the construction of the mother in our culture. "[C]e qu'elle *représente*...dépasse ce qu'elle *est* et elle en *est* irresponsable" (*L'Eden Cinéma* 12). Her role as both victim and instrument of masculine oppression destroys her and harms or destroys her children: "the mother" in Duras' texts shows the futility of maternal love in a matricidal culture.

Notes

[1] The differences between *Un barrage contre le Pacifique* and *L'Eden Cinéma* are primarily related to the different genres; the story is almost identical. Therefore I will confine my comments on *L'Eden Cinéma* to several notes indicating pertinent variations or similarities of language.

[2] In "*L'Eden Cinéma*: Aging and the Imagination in Marguerite Duras," Mary Lydon mentions the first of these definitions in connection with Duras' writings, p. 155. Janice Morgan, speaking about textual transformations in *L'amant*, invokes the third, "Here, personal event has been fully transposed into literature: autobiography has passed into legend" (80), "Fiction and Autobiography/Language and Silence: *The Lover* by Marguerite Duras," in *Redefining Autobiography in Twentieth-Century Women's Fiction*, edited by Janice Morgan and Colette T. Hall. Also see Susan D. Cohen's *Women and Discourse in the Fiction of Marguerite Duras: Love, Legends, Language*. The final chapter is devoted to the concept of "legend" in Duras' work.

[3] Sharon Willis, in *Marguerite Duras: Writing on the Body*, discusses the theme of orality in connection with *L'amante anglaise* and *Moderato cantabile*. See pp. 158–164.

[4] Duras herself has at certain points in her career connected these two. See for example "An Interview with Marguerite Duras" with Susan Husserl-Kapit in which Duras discusses her ideas on "feminine literature."

[5] Marcelle Marini discusses connections between these two writers in *Territoires du féminin*. See pp. 69–75.

[6] This term, which Audre Lorde uses in her text *Zami: a new spelling of my name*, seems admirably suited to Duras' representation of her adolescence.

[7] The importance of this fear is emphasized by an almost exact repetition in *L'Eden Cinéma* : "Je crois qu'elle avait eu peur, la mère, de n'avoir même plus à nous nourrir. Même plus ça" (125). It is worth noting, however, that the change of pronoun from "le" to "nous" indicates an equal concern for her children in the play.

[8] Note that in her chapter "La maladie de la douleur : Duras" in *Soleil noir: dépression et mélancolie*, Julia Kristeva affirms that "Ce sentiment d'abandon inévitable...se noue autour de la figure maternelle" (249). Also Allison Weir, in "Identification with the Divided Mother: Kristeva's Ambivalence," in *Ethics, Politics, and Difference in Julia Kristeva's Writing*, edited by Kelly Oliver, describes the relationship to the mother in Duras' work in this way: "Duras's sad women are walking memories of the hole left by their abandonment, commemorations of the whole that once was. Bodies holding the void inside them, unable to look away, focused always inward on that hole, these women live the melancholy of impossible mourning. For they cannot give up the mother. They keep her absence in their bodies like a wound" (85).

[9] See also Sharon Willis's very interesting development of the connections between the beggar woman, hysteria, and mothers, pp. 25–31.

[10] In *L'Eden Cinéma* the potential of the mother to harm her daughter is alluded to when the mother becomes depressed while the family is in the city. Suzanne recounts:

"Carmen me fait coucher dans sa chambre.
Elle ne veut pas que je couche dans la chambre de la mère.
Elle a peur pour moi" (106–07).

[11] Kevin C. O'Neill, in "Structures of Power in Duras's *Un Barrage contre le Pacifique*," also examines the importance of the gaze in this text.

[12] Also see Marilyn Schuster's discussion of the gaze in *L'amant* in *Marguerite Duras Revisited*, in particular pp. 122–124.

[13] This quotation and the one which precedes it (comparing the view of the face to reading) both help to unsettle the story/history opposition which is consistently deconstructed by this text.

[14] Although the film of *L'amant* directed by Jacques Annaud in 1991 has been rejected by Duras as a false interpretation of her story, it is interesting to compare Annaud's treatment of this almost obsessive positioning of the woman as object of the gaze. While he

follows through on Duras' emphasis on the costume that is worn by the young woman, he does not convey the intensity of the specula(riza)tion in her relationship with her lover that is so notable in the text.

[15]In *The Other Woman: Feminism and Femininity in the Work of Marguerite Duras*, Trista Selous examines the presentation of the narrator of *L'amant* as the object of desire on pp. 192–202.

[16]Marianne Hirsch touches briefly on this question of relative power between the lovers, and on the mother's situation as equally divided: "She is the colonizer, yet, as a woman she is also the colonized." See pp. 151 and 153 in *The Mother/Daughter Plot: Narrative, Psychoanalysis, Feminism*. See also Suzanne Chester in "Writing the Subject: Exoticism/Eroticism in Marguerite Duras's *The Lover* and *The Sea Wall*." This entire essay analyzes the "split in the colonial writing subject" (437). Also see Janine Ricouart's *Ecriture féminine et violence: une étude de Marguerite Duras*. In her third chapter, "Violence envers les enfants et dans le couple," she analyzes the violence between mother and daughter in these autobiographical texts in relation to societal violence. See particularly pp. 89–99.

Chapter V

Writing the Mother-Daughter Story: Narrative Strategies and Thematic Imagery

In this concluding chapter I will discuss the ways in which the differences and similarities in the representation of the mother-daughter relation in the work of Colette, Simone de Beauvoir, and Marguerite Duras contribute to a more general understanding of the "difference" in women's writing. My project is twofold: I hope to show that the similarities in the work of these writers indicate a certain "difference" in women's writing. Yet the many differences between them show that "difference" cannot be seen as monolithic, but rather, varies depending on the writer.

A brief overview of the development of autobiography criticism in the last several decades will be useful to this examination of the representation of the mother-daughter relation in the autobiographies of these three writers.[1] In France as in the United States, the main problem posed by autobiography until approximately twenty years ago was how to distinguish it from other types of writing. Philippe Lejeune's early studies on autobiography, *L'autobiographie en France* and *Le pacte autobiographique*, show this concern as does the work of Elizabeth Bruss in the United States. However, structuralist, deconstructionist, and psychoanalytic theories all began to reshape the ways in which French and Americans understood the interrelations of life and language. These new views seemed particularly useful to an examination of autobiographical writings. Indeed, the questioning of the notions of "self" and "life" that was included in interrogations of language gave prominence to autobiography criticism. For autobiography is founded on the examination of the representation of self, the relation of self to language, the way in which this relation constructs life. Although there are many autobiographies which do not explicitly address these issues, the underlying connections between self and language which structure these texts are congruent with contemporary concerns.

French "feminists" made use of these new formulations of the interrelations of language and society to examine the ways in which gender and language affect each other. The work of Luce Irigaray, among others, indicated the need for a different expression of women's "self." The work of Julia Kristeva, although not necessarily allied with feminist movements, theorized a relation to language in some ways dependent on the early relation to the mother's body. Although in very different ways, these two theoreticians have greatly influenced feminist work in literature as in many other fields.

Yet it is the American feminists, more than the French, who have brought these revisions of language and gender together in a growing number of texts on women's autobiographies.[2] It seems that studies of women's autobiographies follow the earlier studies of autobiography by first focusing on how it is possible to distinguish these from other texts, such as men's autobiographies. Again, autobiography finds itself at the center of many debates. Similarly to the way in which studies of autobiography were well placed for interrogations of the relation of self to language, studies of women's autobiographies necessarily involve questions concerning the possible existence of a "feminine" self.

The determination of the different ways in which a woman might be situated in language is related to important differences within feminist movements. It is often thought that the French feminists who have advocated an *écriture féminine* or *parler-femme*, in other words, those who believe that women need to represent themselves outside of male definitions of "Woman," are suggesting that women are essentially different from men. This is an issue that has occasionally seemed to separate French and American feminisms. However, the debate on essentialism is not so easily located as this would imply. Not all French feminists believe that women's relationship to language is or should be different. Not all Americans disbelieve this. Perhaps even more important, however, is the need to challenge the assumption that this possibly different relation to language essentializes women. Many agree that the way in which women have been constructed makes it very possible that women exist in language differently from men, but that this can be changed.

Another source of debate among feminists is centered on an opposition that is often posited between experience, understood as "reality," and language, which is supposed to transmit this "reality." This opposition has also been used to describe differences between French and American feminists, as well as having been used to distinguish feminist work in the humanities from feminist work in the sciences. Even though both of these polarized views are overly simplified, it is important to acknowledge that the question of whether language is a transparent medium or the basis of our understanding of "reality," articulates some significant differences in feminist thinking. It is true that poststructuralist revisions of subjectivity and individualism do not always seem to answer women's need for agency in their societies. Yet to focus only on the changes needed in social systems seems to ignore the reasons for the inequalities built into these systems. The notion that "difference" is expressed in women's writing is one that needs further examination. The ways in which self-expression affects social structures must not be buried by fears, however understandable, of having to change our understanding of our selves. To study the representation of the "difference" of women's lives is both to learn about what needs to change and to begin to enact this change.

It is important to remember when reading these texts that we are reading transgressors of the Law: women are always rebelling against the patriarchal tradition when they author(ize) their own lives. Not only are women not as encouraged to enter the literary domain as men, but the use of the "paternal tongue" to defy paternal authority often seems to divide women's representations of their selves. Women's self-representation requires as a first step the definition of "self" in a way that is different from the masculine assumption of identity.[3]

When looking at the history of autobiography we find frequent assumptions that all that a woman's autobiography could recount was the story of her life as perceived and validated by the male gaze. The presentation of a self in relation to the other (the reader, for example) can reflect an awareness that the self is changed according to which other it is confronting. Women's positions as both inside and outside the social order, neither the dominant group nor completely excluded from it, mean that their identities are more malleable. These two factors in women's presentation of self, although somewhat enmeshed, are different: a woman's awareness of her unstable positioning in her society and her acknowledgement of the significant influence of the other on her self. The two factors work together to shape women's autobiographies in a different way from men's autobiographies.

One of the most important aspects of the daughter's representation of her relationship with her mother is that it makes more visible the complex and sometimes contradictory creation of the "feminine" in our culture.[4] Freud stated that it is not easy to become a woman; women's autobiographies confirm the truth of his observation, although they may not agree with his reasons. The daughter's recognition of the fact that resemblance to her mother signifies belonging to the gender that is less valued in our culture can be painful, particularly as the mother herself might share in the misogynistic attitudes of her society. The necessity of taking as a model this person who might not like herself or her role can be disturbing. For women, self-love is often complicated by contradictory feelings for the mother.

It would seem that there is a relation between leaving the mother and coming to writing: writing an autobiography could be described as a reenactment of the birth process which emphasizes the daughter's agency rather than the mother's. Each time that she shapes her story she recreates herself, affirming the daughter's authorization of her own life and questioning the role of the mother in the formation of the daughter's subjectivity.

The daughter's juxtaposition of her self to her mother reveals the process that made her who she is and who she is becoming. Whether the daughter appreciates or resents her mother's role, her reaction forms an integral part of her own self-representation. In looking into the mirror that is the autobiographical project, these daughters discover their mothers looking back at them.

Questions of identity and difference are therefore crucial to any examination of the mother-daughter relation, frequently portrayed in women's writing as identities that are both shared and separate. The role of the mother in women's autobiography seems thus to give shape to the subject that is being disclosed through this practice, not quite the writer herself but a fictionalized narrator who is presented as the writer. The presentation of the maternal figure in the stories of Colette, Simone de Beauvoir, and Marguerite Duras structures the reader's understanding of the narrator/subject of the texts, representing the forces, positive or negative, that have shaped her.

In an essay on what she calls "matrocentric" autobiographies, Bella Brodzki describes the mother's role:

> Emblematic of the way language itself obscures and reveals, witholds and endows, prohibits and sanctions, the mother...hovers from within and without. Still powerful and now inaccessible (literally or figuratively), she is the pre-text for the daughter's autobiographical project. (245)

I would add to this that the mother is in some ways the text of the autobiography as it is often by means of the mother that the daughter explains who she is. Feminist theorizing of the pre-oedipal suggests that women's need to separate themselves from their primary caregiver is different from men's individuation. Men turn away from difference; women must turn away from the same. The mirror that Jacques Lacan posits as the mother's representation of the child to herself (i.e., the mother represents a mirroring that precipitates the infant's awareness of self) seems to predominate in the daughter's life. The understanding of self/(m)other that begins in infancy is represented in women's autobiographies as a continuing process.

The pre-oedipal symbiosis, both seductive and terrifying, shows itself in the texts that I have analyzed both as a dream of unity and a memory of traumatic loss. Perhaps these writings give control to the daughters over this lost realm, reassuring them of their separateness while in some ways reaching out for this bond. These contradictory impulses divide the texts, replicating the divisions enunciated within the daughter. The entangled feelings and lives of mother and daughter continue this primary bond, giving it preeminence perhaps over any other bond that the daughter will experience in her life. Indeed, although men are important in the autobiographical writings of Colette, Simone de Beauvoir, and Marguerite Duras, it is not at all certain that they can claim more place in these daughter's emotions than their mothers have. The confusion that sometimes occurs in these texts between mothers and lovers is an important reminder that the mother was, in a sense, the first lover. The original tie to the maternal body can never be entirely eradicated. I believe that the recreation of this body through writing, the inscription of this tie, is one of the reasons for the existence of these texts.

An examination of the mother-daughter relation as it is represented in women's autobiographies helps to elucidate women's relations with other women as well as their own complicity with androcentrism. When speaking of her mother the writer moves from speaking of her own "femininity" to "femininity" in terms of society's construction of the female gender. The mother oscillates in her daughter's representation between an individual with a name and a history or the maternal figure, a shaping force of her daughter's history. The representation of the mother's subjectivity is thus doubly mediated: it is transformed by the daughter's point of view (inasmuch as she can never really articulate the mother's point of view but only try to replicate it), and also by the maternal function: the role that she played in the engenderment of her daughter helps to obscure her own thoughts, feelings, and desires. When women write about their mothers they are inevitably writing about the ambivalence of women's relations to women in an androcentric society. Through the exploration of the mother's subjectivity and subjection, the daughter confronts the double betrayal inherent in the mother-daughter relation: the mother often tries to shape her daughter according to misogynistic values, the daughter often refuses to model herself on this figure who signifies an oppression that the daughter needs to reject.

The tensions of similarity and difference, intimacy and independence structure women's autobiographies in such a way that the writer often seems divided within herself. Indeed there is sometimes a confusion of voices in the texts indicating this struggle: it is not always clear whether the daughter is speaking for herself, or for her mother, or is attempting to transcribe the maternal voice, in some way reproducing her mother. A daughter's identity can thus be pluralized and diffused in her text. Yet this unstable and multivocal identity presents itself in a text which has as a goal the enunciation of the individual life. It seems that the autobiographical project in itself is changed by these circumstances. As the notion of the self becomes more and more destabilized, its representation reflects the impossibility of its enunciation. In some cases women's autobiographies almost state from the beginning the impossibility of the traditional autobiographical project. Writing about the different subject of "autogynography," Domna Stanton notes this apparent contradiction:

> Because of woman's different status in the symbolic order, autogynography...dramatize[s] the fundamental alterity and non-presence of the subject, even as it asserts itself discursively and strives toward an always impossible self-possession. (15)

A different goal thus becomes apparent: a representation of the subject as it has not yet been conceived in Western ontology. The subject of women's autobiography becomes the unspoken and unspeakable, the unknown or unknowable.

A more detailed comparison—first of some of the differences, then of some of the similarities—of the works of these writers will give an idea of the range of emotions and experiences represented by women concerning the(ir) mother. I hope that this will suggest ways of perceiving the mother-daughter bond in these texts which elucidate not only these relations but also the relations of women to their lives in general. Each writer's representation of the maternal function is a commentary on social roles and interactions yet continues to enunciate the particularity of women's lives. The balance between individual and social is thus significant in these texts and it would seem that the mother is placed at the intersection of these two constructs. Without losing sight of the mother's individuality, these daughters still represent her as part of a larger system, a force and a phenomenon of her society. In this way we are reminded that the mother-daughter relation is also a construct, one that operates in every woman's life.

Rewriting history

The different narrative strategies of these writers help to show the various resolutions that women seek to the oppositions of the mother-daughter relation. Colette, Simone de Beauvoir, and Marguerite Duras shaped their autobiographical writings by repeating and revising their stories of childhood and of the transition to adulthood. I would describe this process of re-viewing and re-writing as palimpsest work, in that palimpsests are defined as manuscripts which have been written over several times, with obscured yet still visible traces of earlier writings. It seems to me that this is a useful metaphor for the multiple versions of stories that we find in the autobiographical texts of these writers. Although they cannot efface previously published texts, their retelling is capable of reshaping the reader's understanding of the relationship that is being represented. An examination of the variations within the different versions can give a different understanding of these complex relationships which are, in a sense, triangular: mother, daughter, text. The palimpsestic treatment of these lives has several implications for feminist literary studies. One effect of the retelling and reformulating of these stories is to allow the writer to create herself through building up layers of identity. Yet it is not certain whether this self-representation stabilizes or destabilizes the "self." The process of (re)creation could be seen as a deliberate fragmentation of self, a telling and retelling that challenges the notion of "subject." However the repetitions of palimpsestic texts show that there might be two somewhat oppositional movements in this process. As well as an undoing of the "writing subject," repetition builds up an entity or persona, accruing substance while at the same time refusing unity. There is a subject but it is plural.

In these texts the layers of identity structured by palimpsestic narration give a different shape to the mother's representation. Indeed, these representations acquire a depth of personality that the figure of the mother frequently lacks in literature, often being reduced to a stereotype of a good or bad mother. These writers achieve views of their mothers that are perhaps more complete and more cognizant of the mother's subjectivity than is often the case. In this way the characters that are presented, both mothers and daughters, acquire a new complexity. These characters are shown as contradictory and unfinished. In each case the mother remains other, irreducible, unknowable. Similarly, the relationships that are represented are also processes which seem unending (there is a sense that these writers are carrying on their relationships in writing even after the mother's death) and are not always logically coherent. The multi-faceted vision presented by these writers sometimes fragments an image or an idea, opening up the text to a multiplicity of interpretations or perspectives.

The palimpsestic treatment also foregrounds the unstable division between "fiction" and "autobiography." The writers' revisions of their own life stories continually remind the reader that the notion of objectivity has also been unsettled by the questioning of subjectivity. If the "self" is an unstable entity always undergoing metamorphoses then it follows that history is only a construct of changing points of view and thus mutable itself. Memory is then a creative force and can no longer give to autobiography a factual status withheld from novels. Palimpsest texts undermine concerns with veracity and reveal the impossibility of an unmediated communication of experience. It is this layering or palimpsest of stories which emphasizes being as construct rather than product, a view which is often an important part of women's writing. In this way these autobiographies address a significant issue in contemporary feminist thinking: in demonstrating the construction of personal history, they challenge the notion that "pure" experience can ever be transmitted.

One of the purposes of this study has been to show that the

differences represented in the mother-daughter relation by these writers actually demonstrate various approaches to a central issue both in feminist thinking and in twentieth-century studies: the oppositions of subject and object, and of subjectivity and objectivity. In this analysis of Colette, Simone de Beauvoir, and Marguerite Duras I have shown repeated shifts between the subject and object positions often carried out through the use of both first and third-person narration to describe the life of the writer/narrator. The narrative shifts include multiple points of view: the narrator seems to speak as the child that she is remembering, as the adult who writes the stories of her childhood, and sometimes as/for the mother (this is especially true of Colette, but I think it could also be said for Simone de Beauvoir and Marguerite Duras). In this way the shifts from "I" to "she" sometimes refer to her "present" self and her "former" self, but at other times refer to herself and her mother.

The difference between subjectivity and objectivity, although related to this opposition, is not quite the same. My use of these terms attempts to focus on a narrative strategy that is particularly noticeable in Simone de Beauvoir's writings, yet exists in the work of the other two writers as well: self-characterization versus distantiation. When the narrator positions herself as central to the text, to the events that are taking place, and discusses her thoughts and emotions in relation to these events, she presents herself as another character. However, she also has the possibility of presenting an "objective" distance from the other characters, in this way giving herself a privileged position. The movement from inclusion to separation echoes the movement from subject to object yet works by objectifying the other characters, these semi-real, semi-fictional people that interact with the narrator-character. In this way the writer occasionally participates in and occasionally refutes the objectification that is implied in the writing of an autobiography, the reification of her self and her life. This clearly gives her power, both in her construction of her self, and in her construction of her mother.

Although Colette's writings also play with subjective and objective narration, her method of recounting her memories also emphasizes a strategy of bringing things together, both maintaining differences yet showing areas of differentiation. The layering of stories that we see in *La maison de Claudine*, *La naissance du jour*, and *Sido* challenges concepts of "truth" and "history," suggesting that these are always made up of different viewpoints and therefore infinite. These texts are filled with truths and histories, showing perspectives that merge with and separate from each other.

My study of Colette's texts showed the centrality of an idea of "both/and" which exemplifies her view of herself and her mother: separate yet together. This portrayal of Sido emphasizes the similarities of the two women, occasionally almost merging the two personalities into one in the three texts that I have examined. Often it seems that the only problems that have ever occurred in this relationship were the result of the intrusions of others into this extremely loving dyad. The autobiographical project in this case involves a resurrection of the mother: the focus is on her vitality, her attachment to life, and an affirmation of the fundamental bonds between the two women. After being divided both by life (marriages, geographical distance, etc.) and death the two are reunited in Colette's texts.

Not only does the writer give life to her mother in this way but she creates their bond, representing their importance to each other in her writing. This is not to say that she falsifies (although she adapts or invents her mother's letters to suit her own purposes) but rather to recall that this is, of course, the daughter's point of view. Colette's own freely admitted willingness to merge autobiography with fiction further challenges any attempt to read these texts as a transparent description of this relationship. Rather, Sido becomes more and more transformed in these writings into an emblem of the qualities that Colette has found to be most important to her own life: independence merged with responsibility to others, tenderness merged with a pragmatic view of life, and other qualities give "Sido" the status of a model that goes beyond the individual woman Sido. It is the merging of characteristics that are more commonly seen as opposed which Colette emphasizes in her writing about her mother and which is central to our understanding both of "Sido" and of

"Colette." Colette represents the connections between people, animals, and things as their most important attributes. Her writing is always an exploration of contiguity and affinity, refusing or ignoring polarizations and celebrating joinings. Her autobiography speaks the connections between her self and her mother and, even more, the way in which these extend outward and connect Colette to the world. Her relation to the world is dependent on the umbilical cord forever linking mother and daughter.

In these texts the palimpsest work serves to give new life to the daughter through the mother's recreation: Colette brings her mother back in order to renew herself. She recalls her mother—both remembering her and calling her back into existence—in what seems to be a cycle of self-examination and self-rejuvenation. Writing the daughter's life becomes inseparable from writing the mother into life. The play that we have seen between presence and absence, life and death can be understood as the birth process, in each text transformed so as to give equal importance to maternal and filial author/ity.

La maison de Claudine, *La naissance du jour*, and *Sido* do not so much repeat the same stories as give a range of impressions, often through short anecdotes, of this writer's childhood and her family, particularly of her mother. Although there is relatively little repetition, the effect is of an accumulation of images of Sido and her relationship to her daughter. An example of this is the organization of the stories in *La maison de Claudine*. The temporal shifts between and even within these stories are significant: the first story, "Où sont les enfants," begins with Colette/Gabrielle and her siblings as teenagers but ends with an acknowledgement that many years have passed since this time. "— Où sont les enfants? Deux reposent. Les autres jour par jour vieillissent. S'il est un lieu où l'on attend après la vie, celle qui nous attendit tremble encore, à cause des deux vivants" (9). The following story, "Le sauvage," tells of Sido's marriage to her first husband before the birth of these children. "Amour" is set during Gabrielle's adolescence; in "La petite" and "L'enlèvement" she is younger. "Le curé sur le mur" begins with a conversation between Colette and her own daughter,

Bel-Gazou. These six stories are the first thirty pages of this text; the cumulative effect is of synchrony. The reader has the impression of a continuous "present" which encompasses all of these events and characters. The accumulation is not only of different temporal settings but also of different voices: although Colette generally speaks in the first person, "La petite" is narrated in the third person. Sido is quoted both indirectly and directly. The narrative shifts from "Colette" to "Gabrielle" also give the impression of an accumulation of "presence" as though this character were multiple.

Colette's representation of her self as multiple—multiply named and multiply positioned temporally and textually—takes apart identity only to show it as multi-layered. The narrative shifts from first to third-person narration challenge the distinction between subjectivity and objectivity. It is a vision which is both interior and exterior, attempting to present the self as it is seen and as it is lived.

Both "presence" and "present" are redefined in Colette's writing: in the same way that presence and absence are shown to be an unstable distinction, present and past are perceived as unreliable. The layers of time work with the layering of voices and stories in such a way as to destabilize the relations between writer, text, and reader.

Colette's rewriting of her mother's letters adds to the multivocalness of her writing and to the complexity of her endeavor. She speaks in her mother's voice yet shapes it to say what she wants to say. In this way she seems to create a dialogue between the two women; added into the layers of stories that are recreating her mother is the mother's "own voice," an attempt at transcribing the mother's subjectivity. Bella Brodzki sees this process as an expression of a continuing need for the mother: "[T]hese autobiographical narratives are generated out of a compelling need to enter into discourse with the absent or distant mother" (245–46). This discourse thus balances maternal presence and absence: Colette inscribes her mother's presence, (re)creating her by speaking for her. The mother's voice in Colette's texts can be understood as the speaking of "difference": whether the mother speaking through the daughter or the daughter speaking through the mother, the plurality of the female voice is foregrounded in these texts. In all three texts the language is shaped by the presence of the mother.

Although a central theme of these texts is Sido's love for her family, her garden, and all of nature, the development of this theme shows Sido to be a complex woman, and her relationship to her daughter as far from simple. The narrative technique demonstrates a seeming contradiction: both "Sido" and "Colette" are women who value simplicity yet are not simple themselves. The complexity of the narrative voice and treatment shows these figures to be multi-faceted. Thus the accumulated stories, rather than revealing all that there is to know, only suggest that there will always be more to know.

These texts problematize the notion of "femininity." While at first glance "Sido" would seem to be in many ways a traditional representation of the "feminine"—nurturing, linked to nature, the physical, and the emotional—this figure is not easily categorized. Her strength, independence, and intelligence are in some ways more appropriate to the traditional "masculine" in our culture. Indeed, there is an androgyny in many of Colette's characters which unsettles polarized notions of man and woman. Whether in her descriptions of her mother or herself, Colette often juxtaposes elements of gender roles that are or were more commonly seen as distinct from each other. The instability and arbitrariness to be found in these roles subvert the view of "femininity" as an unquestioned legacy passed from mother to daughter. Rather, in counterpoint to her celebration of her mother is a questioning of the presuppositions that separate maternal from paternal, woman from man. Colette's representation of her own role as a woman frequently stresses the notion of "role."

Colette's work shows a "Sido" who evades attempts to place or define her. The images of a mother who often seems poised to take flight confirm the insubstantiality of the idea of "the mother"; her repeated descriptions of the household utensiles with which Sido is always loaded down suggest that without these weights she would float away. These representations both give substance to her mother and deny the reality of that substance, in the same way that the writer destabilizes her own existence by means of her oscillation between Colette and "Colette." Both creating and demystifying self and (m)other, her texts weave a presence that cannot be clearly located or defined, but is somehow even more present for that very reason.

"Difference" is inscribed in this writing as fluidity. The movements of merging and accumulation which I have described indicate a breaking down of categories, a flowing of one thing into another. Colette's reliance on water imagery—rain, rivers, seas are frequently described—helps to foreground her connections between the "feminine" and the fluid. The merging of mother and daughter is generally presented as just as natural as the joining of two rivers.

Even though Colette's portrayal of Sido and of their relationship is extremely loving, there are still indications that the opposition of the autobiographical "I" to Colette's lyrical "we" is not always without tension. It seems to me that this could be an inherent struggle in matrocentric autobiographies, made even more complex by the irresolvability of the opposition. The writer cannot hope for an eventual victory of either "I" or "we" as in either case the defeat is her own. Clearly a victory of "we" over "I" could signal a dangerous loss of identity, but the opposite case in which the "I" effaces the "we" might be evidence of the effacing of a bond that is necessary to the daughter throughout her lifetime. Total separation is as damaging as total submersion of self in this dyad.

In Colette's autobiographical writing there is often an equilibrium maintained between idyllic merging and necessary individuation. The text shows the subject of this autobiography as a very complex structure: neither completely autonomous nor completely merged, "both/and." It is through palimpsest texts that the daughter succeeds in pluralizing identity without breaking it down completely. The rewriting of the mother and of the daughter —merging and then separating—maintains an "I"/"we" in which we see both characters distinct yet together.

The mother-daughter bond for Simone de Beauvoir is very different from the one that I have just examined. I would suggest that this relationship represents a central sorrow that is never quite healed or resolved. The writer's description of her mother is more clearly connected to Simone de Beauvoir's understanding of women's roles in their society than is the case with Colette: Beauvoir is very aware of the limitations that are responsible for the anger and pain that she describes in her mother's life, yet despite this has difficulty forgiving her. There seems to be a feeling of betrayal on both sides of this relationship due to the fact that the mother knows that she is unhappy yet tries to force her daughter to imitate her, even perhaps resenting her for her ability to escape the destiny that she has accepted.

As in Colette's autobiographies there are two opposed reactions to the mother. Although Beauvoir's distrust and resentment of her mother are easiest to see, her pain at the relative coldness of this relationship is also visible. Not only in *Une mort très douce*, but also in the *Mémoires d'une jeune fille rangée*, there is a poignancy in her description of the loss of the loving relationship of her earliest childhood. *Une mort très douce* also conveys a sense that as well as regretting the relationship that was always strained, she might be recognizing her own suppression of any resemblances between the two women. In *A Poetics of Women's Autobiography*, Sidonie Smith describes one potential choice of a woman autobiographer as a "patrilineal contract," which is to identify herself with the father and his power: she "silences that part of herself that identifies her as a daughter of her mother" (53). This is how I would tend to see Beauvoir's texts yet the fact that her mother has a much more important role in her writing than her father indicates the occasional emergence of the matrilineal, breaking through the father's language.

In *Mémoires d'une jeune fille rangée* and *Une mort très douce*, Simone de Beauvoir would seem to emphasize opposition both in her view of her self and her mother and in the relation of these two texts to each other. Although there are many points of agreement between the texts (as, indeed, there are between the writer and her mother), what is foregrounded is difference. An oppositional movement can be seen in her descriptions of men and women, in her views of herself and her mother, in her reactions to her mother. The two texts are also in opposition to each other in form: the first is a traditional narration of the steps from infancy to adulthood, the second a more fragmented recital of the change in self-awareness that takes place when a parent dies (particularly the parent whose example has been more significant).

In some cases the second text repeats the first yet changes surround these repetitions, unsettling their meanings. Although the stories might be very much the same, they are told differently and this reshapes them. In the *Mémoires*, the view of the mother often shows her to be a person of extremes: "Si un de ses intimes la contrariait ou l'offensait, elle réagissait souvent par la colère et par de violents éclats de franchise. En société cependant, elle demeura toujours timide" (51). In *Une mort très douce* the representations of the mother tend to be much less juxtapositional: "[D]otée d'un tempérament robuste et ardent, elle s'était détraquée et rendue incommode par ses renoncements. Alitée, elle avait décidé de vivre pour son compte et elle gardait cependant un constant souci d'autrui: de ses conflits était née une harmonie" (148–49). The resolution of conflicts that Simone de Beauvoir describes as having taken place in her mother is occasionally echoed in the re-visions of this relationship between the two women, or what I would call palimpsest work, that we see in the later text.

The change in perspective is due, at least in part, to the mother's death which occurs between the two texts, freeing the writer to speak more openly and providing her with an opportunity to reflect on her mother's life and on their relationship in a different way. Even if she does not significantly change stated events (in fact, as opposed to the autobiographical writings of both Colette and Duras, Beauvoir's texts are presented as being as truthful and factual as possible), her view has been modified in certain ways. The admission of how deeply affected she had been by her mother's death is an acknowledgement of a connection between the two women which earlier could have been threatening.

Yet despite the modifications in the view of the mother after her death, Beauvoir continues to emphasize the differences between them as if to show once again that her decision to become in some ways the opposite of her mother was necessary. For Beauvoir the autobiographical project involves self-defense in both of its meanings: she defends the choices that she has made in her life and she defends herself from her mother, from her mother's example. The two texts both show a fear of resembling the mother. The autobiography becomes a wall to be placed around the "I" both affirming its existence and protecting it. There is very little "we" in these two texts, although the mother-daughter relationship is presented as less hostile in *Une mort très douce*. Rather than "we," Beauvoir's descriptions of events are often phrased as "I" versus "she," suggesting an adversarial relation between mother and daughter. Her surprise at her reaction to her mother's final illness and death demonstrate the distance between the two women even though suggesting that there are aspects of their feelings for each other that the daughter has not clearly understood.

In the first text the role of the mother as primary shaper of her daughter's "femininity" is clearly enunciated. Beauvoir discusses her mother's influence on her formation as a woman as well as showing the oppositions that her parent's roles represent for her. Her choice is not only for the father but against the mother: not only is she attracted to her father's freedom and power, she is repelled by her mother's dependence and weakness. The man/woman opposition is central in these two texts and it seems that it is crucial to Beauvoir's self-view to show these roles as clearly polarized. The autobiographical project is inseparable from the understanding of gender roles in the case of this writer. Her difficult connection to her mother links these two endeavors: explaining who her mother is explains who she is (primarily by opposition) and helps to explain her view of "femininity."

Although the representation of the mother in each of these texts is used to explain the daughter, the repetition and revision reflect the writer's continuing self-evaluation. Oppositions are not only between self and (m)other, but also between self and previous self, showing more divisions within the daughter in the later text than in the earlier. The mother's death has modified the more clear-cut oppositions of *Mémoires* and perhaps troubled the daughter's self-view, but the representation of the mother is still shaped by the daughter's wariness of this person and of her role. The alternating views of self and other seem occasionally to begin to collapse when Beauvoir speaks of herself and her mother, yet she continues to insist on this crucial distinction (even if she no longer completely believes in it).

This textual reconstruction of the mother posits itself as an objective presentation of that person yet it is necessarily more. The two texts could be described as opposing two different ideas of autobiography: as a literary creation or as an historical account. For although Beauvoir presents these texts as factual recitations of events, we have seen that there are occasionally images or descriptions which shift the reader's attention from the events to their textualization, reminding the reader that writing is always creation. Beauvoir's project is not reducible to *reportage*, her inscription of this relationship shapes it according to multiple purposes.

The distantiation that was noted in her two texts is an important aspect of her writing of her self. The narrative movements from omniscient and supposedly objective narration to subjective involvement indicate the daughter's need to recreate her self through the text, separate and distinct from the other characters that she describes so lucidly. Thus we see a self that is created in alternating movements, shifting from subjectivity to objectivity. Although the same narrative strategy was noted in Colette's work, the effect is different. Colette showed a narrator who could move from inside a character to outside, merging different views. Beauvoir's narrative shifts impose distance between her self and the characters that she describes. Her descriptions of her emotions are followed by an analysis of these feelings, asserting her difference from the others who are presented as incapable of the same reasoning, and her distance from the events that she is describing.

The relation to the mother is shown as painful and forever unresolved. It would seem that Beauvoir's rejection of her mother requires that she reject certain parts of herself. Her autobiographical writings show a strong daughter opposed to a weak mother yet at the same time they show that the connections between them are very important. It is possible that Beauvoir's consciousness of this undermines a more predominant need to distance her self from her mother and in some ways unsettles her representation of her relations to her mother, leaving spaces in her texts where more could be said.

Simone de Beauvoir shows her self as split. The oppositions that she shows between her parents and between gender roles are oppositions that cut across her life as a woman. The self-representation in these texts is necessarily divided; not only is there a shift between the two texts but particularly in the later text the reader can see movements of identification and repulsion which indicate the ambivalence in this writer not only toward her mother but toward her own identity.

In a sense the writing of the self in these texts could be seen as a betrayal against which Beauvoir struggles. The need to separate from the mother not only refuses the mother's life but implicates the daughter in the mother's death. In an attempt to give birth to her own self-determined subjectivity, Beauvoir writes her distance from the maternal body, interposing words between her self and her mother.[5] The writing of the mother's death in some ways both confirms and subverts her attempt at individuation. It would seem that she discovers in this process that the mother is forever a part of her which cannot be denied.

Thus in these texts we could see the writing of "difference" as a tension between the paternal and the maternal tongues. The ambivalence that Simone de Beauvoir expresses toward her mother and toward her own "femininity" shows itself in an alternating movement in her language. In her representation of a split self—man/woman, I/she—"difference" is voiced. In these texts difference between men and women is both accepted and struggled against. Simone de Beauvoir's alliance with the masculine intellectual community fragments her views of herself and of other women. "Difference" becomes the site of her own divisions.

The maternal figure in *Un barrage contre le Pacifique, L'Eden*

Cinéma, L'amant, and *L'amant de la Chine du Nord* is represented as a site of contradictions. She is an almost overwhelming force yet at the same time her defeat and madness suggest an absence rather than a presence to be struggled against: at times she is presented as almost mechanical, repeating the same words, going through the same motions despite their uselessness or lack of logic. It is this frightening lack of self that the daughter must avoid; faced with her mother's emptiness she must show herself to be different, to be someone. The autobiographical project vacillates, showing both the horror and the adoration that the mother inspires in her daughter, claiming both difference and complicity in their relationship. In Duras' descriptions a blurring of boundaries is presented as an abyss, emblematic of her relationship with her mother.

The revisions in these four texts show a subtle shifting of presentation and perspective that enunciates what could be described as an *entre-deux*. This is different from the alternating movement that structures Beauvoir's work and it is also different from the merging or "both/and" of Colette's texts: it is the vertiginous hesitation between two subjectivities which is abjection. The *entredeux* is evidenced in the mother-daughter relation, in the shifts between one text and another, and, more specifically than in the work of the other two writers, in the subject/object opposition. Indeed, Duras' work deliberately questions distinctions and categories that are more commonly accepted: not only self and (m)other, but story and history are shown to have indistinct boundaries as well. "C'est fini, je ne me souviens plus. C'est pourquoi j'en écris si facile [de ma mère] maintenant, si long, si étiré, elle est devenue écriture courante" (*L'amant* 38).

The autobiographical project in these texts is multiple, reflecting the divisions of the subject that is represented. However, I would suggest that the representation of absence figured by the abyss of the mother-daughter relation shapes this writing. In this sense these texts are/are not about the writer and her mother: the subversion of the signifier-referent relation is an important aspect of their postmodernism. Yet in as much as Duras uses events of her life (validated by concrete documentation such as photographs) to enact this challenge to referentiality, the subject of the text flickers in and out of existence.

The palimpsestic work is very clear in these texts. In each telling of her story she explicitly modifies it to achieve a different effect. Each time the portrayal of the girl is different, as is the portrayal of the mother and of their relationship. The emphasis is on emotion rather than fact, on the landscape of the psyche rather than on history. As the stories are interwoven, so the mother-daughter relationship seems to be an entangling of two personalities that are not completely separate. The daughter's view of self and (m)other is unfinished like the story, there is no resolution. Her representation of their relationship emphasizes hopeless love; even more tragic than the impossibility of the relationship between the girl and her lover is the impossibility of her ever feeling loved by her mother as she needs to feel. The reiteration of words and phrases in these texts gives a sense of inexorable destiny; although details of the story change, the essential is the same, there is no evolution. Duras mythicizes her life in this way and gives her relationship with her mother central place in all of the writings of the myth.

Thus repetition in the work of Marguerite Duras seems only to emphasize the immutability of this relation. The mother cannot help herself or her daughter. The daughter's only hope for survival might be to distance herself from her mother. Yet despite the distance that she imposes, the mother returns again and again in her writing. The daughter presents herself as haunted by her mother, haunted by the failure of their relationship. The death of the mother means among other things that the relationship can never be changed for the better (except perhaps in writing), the daughter is forced to try to accept her loss. Duras returns repeatedly to the tale of how she became a woman both like and unlike her mother. Each telling conveys more of the rage and pain that were her legacy from her mother yet paradoxically each telling softens the representation of the mother, becoming more sympathetic despite the continuing anger. Although the mother is gradually made a more positive figure, there is no forgiveness in these texts; there is understanding but never acceptance of what has taken place.

Duras links her mother's life to a "feminine" condition of victimization showing not only the connections between herself and her mother, but between all women. As in Simone de Beauvoir's work, "woman" has a political specificity yet her presentation is very different. For Duras there is no choice between masculine or feminine power; her bond with her mother is affirmed both by their relation as mother and daughter and by the more general relation of women together. Although in these autobiographical writings she does not suggest that women should take political action, the recognition of women's lack of power is an important part of these texts.

The mother's role in her daughter's "femininity" is also very ambiguously described, although important. Her attitude toward her daughter's sexuality is unpredictable: she vacillates between her interest in profiting from her daughter's relationship with a wealthy man and her fury at the dishonor that this has brought to the family. Although in general she does not appear to instruct her daughter concerning her role as a woman, the daughter's conception of this role is clearly formed by her mother's (for the most part negative) example. In this sense Duras does not present her mother as responsible for her except that her example serves as a warning to the daughter so that she might learn to fight her oppressors with more success than her mother had.

While showing her fear of the mother and of becoming like her, Duras also shows her admiration and sorrow for her. Indeed, the writing of these texts serves both as a public vindication of her mother and as a denunciation of those who destroyed her. Even the mother's madness which is emphatically described and affirmed is somewhat contradictorily labeled a fabrication of her oppressors, reminding her readers that women who have tried to contend with patriarchal authority have been silenced with accusations of madness throughout the centuries. In a sense, the contradiction fades away when we reflect on women's inside/outside position in the patriarchy: being outside masculine logic woman is always by definition mad. The mother in Duras' texts is/is not mad.

The repeated yet different story of *Un barrage contre le*

Pacifique, *L'Eden Cinéma*, *L'amant*, and *L'amant de la Chine du Nord* is a very condensed autobiographical statement. Duras takes the events of approximately two years and tells them over and over, adjusting details, emphasis, tone, characters. This period is used to encapsulate what it was for her to become an adult woman. There is a sense that everything that there is to know about her can be understood from this story. In this way her autobiography challenges the more common notion of the individual who develops in a linear evolution, presenting the change from child to adult as a moment's decision, arrived at by chance and then endured. This autobiography shows a rupture rather than a process. It is possible that the image of the abyss which I used to describe this mother-daughter relation could also describe the entry into adulthood for Duras. This image also represents the use of language in these texts which are seemingly organized around blanks—on the page, in the story, in the memory of the narrator—opening the story to emptiness and incompletion.

This autobiography is in many ways about loss of self; the narration slips back and forth between "I" and "she," referring to the girl who is the central character in both first and third-person, or referring to the narrator and her mother. Thus one aspect of the daughter's legacy from her mother is an unstable or dispersed identity which in many ways fractures the autobiographical text. There is a writing of the self into and out of existence which perhaps echoes the cycles of creation and destruction which seem to have shaped this childhood. There is a sense that Duras sees herself as doomed to be her mother's daughter, sharing a destiny that is inescapable.

These texts do not so much show a re-birth, as a re-construction of self. The self is shown to be in fragments that can be disassembled and reassembled in different ways. Duras re-examines the common understanding of the mother as giver of life to her child. In this autobiography life is a continual struggle to recreate oneself away from the mother and her violence and madness. Each writing gives the daughter more power in individuation, yet the self in these texts is shown to exist only in relation to another. There is a continual shift between self-subject and self-object, insisting on the possibility of being simultaneously subject/object. The movement of subjectivity between self and other is presented primarily through sight, in a sense preserving "self" from dispersal through visual objectification.

Duras' writing embodies "difference." The slippage of signifiers, the fragmentation of the subject, the disruption of chronological time all confront "masculine" logic and inscribe the "feminine" in these texts. The repetition of this story can be seen as layers of representation, each representation of her self undoing without eradicating the previous representation. The emphasis on multiplicity is seen both in the subjects of these texts and in the texts themselves. "Difference" is presented as destabilization: it unseats notions of the unified subject and history, and it subverts closure. The "feminine" self is multiple, autogenic, and unending.

Redefining self

The similarities between Colette, Simone de Beauvoir, and Marguerite Duras are somewhat easier to enunciate than their differences. Their views of themselves have many commonalities and their representations of their relationships with their mothers also share certain attributes. Each writer shows a concern with the self/other opposition which manifests itself in movements of attraction and repulsion for the mother. Although these movements are not exactly alike in each writer, they demonstrate ambivalent, if not contradictory, feelings for the maternal figure. Each uses her "mother," this character that she presents to the reader, to show her self—what she is and what she is not. The "mother" is thus alternately a mirror in which the writer sees herself and an inversion of her self-view, representing her fears, uncertainties, and choices. It is through this reflection or contrast that the reader can see some of the decisions that women must make.

The motif/symptoms which I have examined in previous chapters can be seen as indicative of both the longings and the terrors that seem almost inevitably to exist in these relationships. In each case these symptoms showed what could be called two voices: they spoke the enduring importance of the mother-daughter bond yet they also spoke the need to finish with the mother. These motifs could be understood as the speech of the hysteric speaking through these texts. Hysteria has been defined as a "maladie par représentation,"[6] and I would suggest that hysterical speech, which is so often corporeal speech, is here used to articulate the maternal body. That is to say that these motif/symptoms speak the repressed body of the mother in the writings of these women's lives. In each case the motifs have shown a certain unease in the writer's view of herself which is not directly addressed but rather shows itself only to be covered over or evaded in some way.

This view of the motifs would indicate a further analogy to the language of psychoanalysis. It is possible that the daughters are representing through a process of condensation the insistent presence of the maternal figure in their lives. If we understand condensation as an accumulation of signifiers which are used metaphorically, it can be seen in these texts as overdetermined motifs which represent in ways that are interrelated the connection to and repression of the maternal body.[7]

Condensation occurs as an attempt to evade the censorship which comes about as a result of primary repression. This censorship is described as a function "qui se révèle par des <<blancs>> ou des altérations, de passages tenus pour inacceptables."[8] The texts of these three writers have been shown in some ways to be founded on "blanks." Not only the silence so central to Beauvoir's writings on her mother, but the gaps of Duras' story, and Colette's concealment of her self in language all indicate the presence of prohibition. Their shared silence is based on *the* secret: desire of the mother. This could be another function of the palimpsest work: what is covered over or effaced is a sexual rapport that is perhaps our culture's most prohibited desire. If the mother-daughter relation is, as Irigaray says, "le continent noir du continent noir," it would follow that any hint of desire in this repressed or denied relation must be repressed or denied as well.

We could agree with Roland Barthes that the maternal body is every writer's (revealed) secret when s/he writes, yet the presence and repression of the mother in these texts seem to be related to issues of identity that are different for daughters. Some psychoanalytic theoreticians would suggest that a man is forbidden by the Law to return to his mother's body yet cannot stop wanting it, whereas the woman is saved by the Law from this return which would mean loss of her self. These autobiographical texts make use of the paternal language to speak the connection to the maternal, perhaps protected by the language itself.

As we saw in the analysis of Colette's works, the motifs of mourning and jealousy indicate a concern with maternal presence, an ambivalence directed at maternal *jouissance*, and an attraction to the mother which acknowledges the possibility of mother-daughter desire. Both the imagery and the structure of Colette's texts are seductive, drawing the reader into a realm of maternal plenitude and pleasure. Yet at the same time there is an awareness of the dangers of this realm, one of these dangers being that it is impermanent. The realm of the maternal is presented both as ideal and more real than real, absent yet omnipresent. Through themes of mourning and jealousy this writer simultaneously gives her mother up and claims her for herself. These symptoms speak a connection that can never be repressed and which will always trouble women in that they must live with paternal law.

Silence and complicity in Simone de Beauvoir's writings speak divided loyalties and shared betrayals. This writer's ambivalence concerning the role of her mother in her life continues into her descriptions of her mother's death bed. The fact that the ambivalence concerns her own role in society as well is clear in her need to establish categories, affirm dichotomies, maintain distinctions. We could say that these texts are an attempt to silence the maternal body but an attempt that fails because of the impossibility of the task. The silence is alternately imposed on her mother and herself, her complicity is dual as well, divided between compliance with the paternal law and connection to the maternal body. Beauvoir seems to search for resolution but can only show divisions: the motif/symptoms speak a repression which splits her in pieces.

Marguerite Duras shows the relation to the mother to be founded on fear of attack from within and without. Her mother seems both to engulf her and to live within her. The motifs of orality and specularity show the struggle to separate from the mother's body as impossible yet it is equally impossible to stop struggling. In this relation both subjectivity and sanity are continually at stake and the daughter fights to establish a consciousness of her self. Yet she also shows an adhesion to her mother which indicates that her fight is with herself as well. Ambivalence is predominant in Duras' representations of this relation, sometimes seeming to give almost every statement about her mother a dual meaning. In their reference to the earliest contacts with the mother these symptoms evince a dual consciousness, that which the mother and child share in the first months of life.

Whether the end of the pre-oedipal relation to the mother is described as the entry into language, knowledge of the penis, submission to the Law of the Father, or recognition of the mother's desire, it would seem that this time of transition is different for women. In fact this time is the first recognition of difference: difference between self and other, and difference between the mother and the father. For women, the recognition of the self/other split is accompanied by the realization of a split that puts self and mother on one side and the possessor of power on the other side. The awareness of self as distinct from other is thus accompanied by the awareness of self as less powerful if not powerless.

It would seem that one manner of resisting this double loss is to make use of the language of loss to try to reclaim some possibility of power in the paternal realm. Yet this is a project that brings further separation. For although they succeed in finding a voice, it seems that their language separates them even more from the maternal body. It also seems that the voice has less validity than that of men writers and so the possibility of more power is illusory or at least incomplete. Thus the notion of betrayal that seems to enter into the texts that I have examined. The use of the father's language helps to repress the mother whether or not that is the purpose of the daughter's writing. Yet what choice is she given? Silence or betrayal, death or mutilation.

Thus the hysterical body which speaks through these texts can be seen in various ways. In Colette's texts this could be seen as denial of loss and admission of desire, in the writings of Simone de Beauvoir there is a struggle for and against silence which is founded on the acknowledgment of a dual complicity, Duras shows possession and objectification as necessary aspects of maternal identification. The struggle for individuation often seems almost physical, yet it is language and gaps in language which must convey it.

Women's need to turn away from their mothers for individuation often becomes a turning against them for self-protection. Yet this rejection is ultimately self-destructive in that women who are distant from their mothers are often distanced from themselves: "The daughter cannot escape the mother without disempowering the mother and herself as woman" (Smith, "The Impact of Critical Theory" 5). These autobiographies demonstrate the problems of female bonding, the needs and fears that invest it. In showing how difficult it is they also give an idea of how important it is; the struggle for and against intimacy are intertwined. In these texts the mother is always the Other against/through whom each woman perceives herself.

It is the mother's example which makes these women aware of the contradictions inherent in the "feminine" role. In attempting to live these contradictions, perhaps in a less self-destructive manner, each daughter is forced in some way to refuse her mother, not just her mother's life but who her mother is. In this way the daughter's autobiography must always demonstrate the closeness between the two (in showing her mother's influence) and the distance (in showing how she has rejected, at least partially, that influence). The mother as model figures the masochism required for women to accept their roles in society yet at the same time can represent the strength that comes from adapting and surviving these roles. The texts that I have examined show the distance established between women by their participation in a misogynistic culture.

A dominant theme in these texts is contradiction, particularly in the representation of the mother. In the same way that it is impossible to see oneself as others do, it is perhaps the case that the mother and daughter identities are so entangled that one cannot see one's mother in the way that others are seen. It is a view always refracted through the view of the self and similarly to the view of the self, fictionalized.

There is therefore an interchange: while the view of the self is originally shaped by the view of the mother, the view of the mother can only be transmitted through the daughter's eyes. Indeed, the mother/mirror imagery that I have made use of in my analysis of women's autobiography requires further examination. The mother in these texts can only reflect the daughter's imposition of her own view. In other words, if a mother's face appears in the mirror, it is the daughter's vision of herself which put it there. The concept of the mother as mirror will always relegate the mother to the position of object, rather than subject. It is not certain that it is ever possible for a woman to see her mother as an independent person, the subject of her own life. These writers are capable of temporarily distancing themselves from their mothers long enough to give an approximate idea of what their thoughts, feelings, and desires might have been. Yet this greater objectivity still tends to collapse into objectification.

Both the autobiographical and the theoretical texts that I have made use of show the tension that results from the continued connection to the maternal body and a denial of this body. Whether addressed directly by Kristeva and Irigaray, or represented more indirectly by Colette, Beauvoir, and Duras, absence is omnipresent in these texts. The self/other opposition which is emphasized by all five writers is itself a symptom of the disruption of identity which is caused by the attempt to construct the mother as Other, always undermined by the insistent presence of the mother in the daughter's psyche.

Representing "difference"

For each of the writers that have been analyzed here—Colette, Simone de Beauvoir, Marguerite Duras—we have seen "difference" represented as movements between different positions. The texts that I have examined show movements of merging and separation in women's writing, replicating the movements of attraction and repulsion which structure the mother-daughter relation, showing women to be both pluralized and fragmented by their connections to their mothers.

The figures of "difference" that I have identified in these writings—fluidity, division, destabilization—help us to see that although women writers might perceive the mother-daughter relationship in similar ways there are still significant differences among them. Some writers emphasize merging, others the need for separation, some see the two movements as equally important.

The work of the theoreticians Luce Irigaray and Julia Kristeva foregrounds the ambivalence in the mother-daughter relation, explaining it in part, yet not completely. Although it is the theoretical texts that ask the most direct questions about the mother-daughter relation, perhaps the closest that we can come to answers at this time are in the autobiographical texts. For these autobiographies bring together politics and the psyche, society and the individual. Each writer has her own views on how the balance of power could be shifted. Colette's texts affirm the power of women's connections among themselves, Beauvoir denounces the inequality of man-woman relations, Duras affirms the resilient power of the "feminine." The palimpsest work reveals areas of discomfort or uncertainty, both pain and desire. The rewriting of one's life, the re-presentation of the mother-daughter relation, allows for an attempt at resolution yet at the same time shows the impossibility of an ending to this story.

The daughters in these texts repeatedly write their mothers into existence, thus carrying out a dichotomized strategy of self-realization. The use of the father's language to make present the mother's body is the basis of the "both/and," the alternation, the *entre-deux* that these writers must both write and live to be the daughters of both parents, to be women who are not simply not-men, to escape "indifference."

Notes

[1] For an excellent and detailed analysis of the history of autobiography criticism, see chapters 1 and 2 of Elisabeth Mantello's "L'autobiographie dérangée."

[2] See Shari Benstock, *The Private Self: Theory and Practice of Women's Writing;* Bella Brodzki and Celeste Schenck, *Life/Lines: Theorizing Women's Autobiography*; Leigh Gilmore, *Autobiographics: A Feminist Theory of Women's Self-Representation*; Françoise Lionnet, *Autobiographical Voices: Race, Gender, Self-Portraiture*; Sidonie Smith, *A Poetics of Women's Autobiography* and *Subjectivity, Identity, and the Body: Women's Autobiographical Practices in the Twentieth Century*; and Domna Stanton, *The Female Autograph* for examples of recent American feminist studies of autobiography.

[3] Shoshana Felman, in *What Does a Woman Want? Reading and Sexual Difference*, describes the difference that I am addressing in this way: "I will suggest that *none of us, as women, has as yet, precisely, an autobiography.* Trained to see ourselves as objects and to be positioned as the Other, estranged to ourselves, we have a story that by definition cannot be self-present to us, a story that, in other words, is not a story, but *must become* a story" (14).

[4] See, however, Shirley Neuman's excellent analysis of the importance of the mother in women's *and* men's autobiographies titled "'Your Past...Your Future': Autobiography and Mother's Bodies," in *Genre—Trope—Gender*, pp. 53–86, edited by Barry Rutland.

[5] Mari H. O'Brien also suggests, in "My (M)other, (My)self: Textual Maternity and Self Propagation in Simone de Beauvoir's *Mémoires d'une jeune fille rangée*," that by writing her autobiography Beauvoir "substitute[s] a linguistic maternity for a biological one" (177).

[6] See Laplanche and Pontalis, *Vocabulaire de la psychanalyse*, pp. 177–79.

[7] Jacques Lacan discusses condensation in "L'instance de la lettre dans l'inconscient ou la raison depuis Freud" in *Ecrits I*.

[8] *Vocabulaire de la psychanalyse,* p. 63.

Bibliography

Simone de Beauvoir

Ascher, Carol. *Simone de Beauvoir: A Life of Freedom.* Boston: Beacon Press, 1981.

Bair, Deirdre. "'My Life...This Curious Object': Simone de Beauvoir on Autobiography." *New York Literary Forum* 12–13 (1984): 237–245.

Beauvoir, Simone de. *Le deuxième sexe.* 1949. Paris: Gallimard Folio/Essais, 1976.

——. *Mémoires d'une jeune fille rangée.* Paris: Gallimard, 1958.

——. *Une mort très douce.* Paris: Gallimard Folio, 1964.

Clément, Catherine. "Les pelures du réel." *Magazine Littéraire* 145 (février 1979): 25–27.

Dayan, Josée, and Malka Ribowska. *Simone de Beauvoir. Un film de Josée Dayan et Malka Ribowska avec la participation de Jean-Paul Sartre, Claude Lanzmann, Jacques Laurent et Olga Bost.* Paris: Gallimard, 1980.

Evans, Mary. *Simone de Beauvoir: A Feminist Mandarin.* London: Tavistock, 1985.

Fuchs, Jo-Ann P. "Female Eroticism in *The Second Sex.*" *Feminist Studies* 6.2 (1980): 304–313.

Kadish, Doris Y. "Simone de Beauvoir's *Une mort très douce*: Existential and Feminist Perspectives on Old Age." *The French Review* 62.4 (1989): 631–639.

MacDonald, Marylea. "Le Pacte Autobiographique dans les *Mémoires* de Simone de Beauvoir." *Simone de Beauvoir Studies* 9 (1992): 75–79.

MacKeefe, Deborah. "Zaza Mabille: Mission and Motive in Simone de Beauvoir's Memoires." *Contemporary Literature* 24.2 (1983): 204–221.

Mantello, Elisabeth Lucette Roberte. "L'Autobiographie dérangée: *Mémoires d'une jeune fille rangée* de Simone de Beauvoir, *La Bâtarde* de Violette Leduc." *DAI* 48.1 (1987): 138A. University of Wisconsin.

Marks, Elaine, ed. *Critical Essays on Simone de Beauvoir.* Boston: G. K. Hall, 1987.

——. *Simone de Beauvoir: Encounters with Death.* New Brunswick: Rutgers University Press, 1973.

Moi, Toril. "Existentialism and Feminism: the Rhetoric of Biology in *The Second Sex*." *Oxford Literary Review* 8.1–2 (1986): 88–95.

——. *Feminist Theory and Simone de Beauvoir.* Oxford: Basil Blackwell, 1990.

O'Brien, Mari H. "My (M)other, (My)self: Textual Maternity and Self-Propagation in Simone de Beauvoir's *Mémoires d'une jeune fille rangée*." *Cincinnati Romance Review* 13 (1994): 173–81.

——. "Reading the Text, Writing the Self: Beauvoir's and Sartre's Intertextual Adventures in Androcentric Language." *CEA Critic* 57.1 (Fall 1994): 77–88.

"Simone de Beauvoir: Witness to a Century." Special Issue of *Yale French Studies* 72 (1986).

Tegyey, Gabriella. "Mères et filles chez Simone de Beauvoir." *Acta Litteraria Academiae Scientiarum Hungaricae* 32.1–2 (1990): 133–141.

Yalom, Marilyn. "They Remember Maman: Attachment and Separation in Leduc, de Beauvoir, Sand, and Cardinal." *Essays in Literature* 8.1 (1981): 73–90.

Zerelli, Linda M.G. "A Process without a Subject: Simone de Beauvoir and Julia Kristeva on Maternity." *Signs: Journal of Women in Culture and Society* 18.1 (Autumn 1992): 111–135.

Colette

Barbour, Sarah. "*La Naissance du jour* by Colette: Who is this Woman Writing?" *Australian Journal of French Studies* 27.3 (Sept.–Dec. 1990): 242–253.

Bernard, Bray, ed. *Colette: nouvelles approches critiques.* Paris: Nizet, 1986.

Colette. *La maison de Claudine*. Paris: Hachette, 1960.
——. *La naissance du jour*. Paris: Garnier-Flammarion, 1984.
——. *Sido*. Paris: Hachette, 1961.
Eisinger, Erica Mendelson, and Mari Ward McCarty, eds. *Colette: The Woman, the Writer*. University Park: Pennsylvania State University Press, 1981.
Flieger, Jerry Aline. *Colette and the Fantom Subject of Autobiography*. Ithaca: Cornell University Press, 1992.
Fraiman, Susan D. "Shadow in the Garden: The Double Aspect of Motherhood in Colette." *Perspectives on Contemporary Literature* 11 (1985): 46–53.
Huffer, Lynne R. *Another Colette: The Question of Gendered Writing*. Ann Arbor: University of Michigan Press, 1992.
Jouve, Nicole Ward. *Colette*. Bloomington: Indiana University Press, 1987.
——. "Oranges et sources: Colette et Hélène Cixous." *Hélène Cixous, chemins d'une écriture*. Ed. Françoise van Rossum-Guyon and Myriam Díaz-Diocaretz. Saint-Denis: Presses Universitaires de Vincennes, 1990. 55–73.
Ladimer, Bethany. "A Sick Child and a Cure: Mother-Daughter Relations in Colette." *Genders* 6 (1989): 74–87.
——. "Moving Beyond Sido's Garden: Ambiguity in Three Novels by Colette." *Romance Quarterly* 36.2 (1989): 153–167.
Lastinger, Valérie. "*La Naissance du jour*: la désintégration du 'moi' dans un roman de Colette." *French Review* 61.4 (March 1988): 542–551.
Lilienfeld, Jane. "The Magic Spinning Wheel: Straw to Gold— Colette, Willy, and Sido." *Mothering the Mind*. Ed. Ruth Perry and Martine Watson Brownley. New York: Holmes and Meier, 1984. 164–178.
Marks, Elaine. *Colette*. New Brunswick: Rutgers University Press, 1960.
Milner, Christiane. "Le corps de Sido." *Europe* 631–32 (Nov.-Dec. 1981): 71–84.
Tinter, Sylvie. "Sidonie Colette ou le temps de la mère." *Etudes Art et Littérature Université de Jerusalem* 14 (Printemps 1987):

33–47.

Marguerite Duras

Ames, Sanford Scribner, ed. *Remains to be Seen: Essays on Marguerite Duras*. New York: Peter Lang, 1988.

Armel, Aliette. *Marguerite Duras et l'autobiographie*. France: Le Castor Astral, 1990.

Bajomée, Danielle, and Ralph Heyndels, eds. *Ecrire dit-elle: imaginaires de Marguerite Duras*. Brussels: Editions de l'Université de Bruxelles, 1985.

Borgomano, Madeleine. *Duras: une lecture de fantasmes*. Belgium: Cistre-Essais, 1985.

———. "Une écriture féminine? A propos de Marguerite Duras." *Littérature* 53 (February 1984): 59–68.

———. *L'écriture filmique de Marguerite Duras*. Paris: Albatros, 1985.

Chester, Suzanne. "Writing the Subject: Exoticism/Eroticism in Marguerite Duras's *The Lover* and *The Sea Wall*." *De/Colonizing the Subject: The Politics of Gender in Women's Autobiography*. Ed. Sidonie Smith and Julia Watson. Minneapolis: University of Minnesota Press, 1992. 436–457.

Cohen, Susan D. *Women and Discourse in the Fiction of Marguerite Duras: Love, Legends, Language*. Amherst: University of Massachusetts Press, 1993.

Duras, Marguerite. *L'amant*. Paris: Editions de Minuit, 1984.

———. *L'amant de la Chine du Nord*. Paris: Gallimard, 1991.

———. *Un barrage contre le Pacifique*. Paris: Gallimard, 1950.

———. *L'Eden Cinéma*. 1977. Paris: Mercure de France-Folio, 1986.

———. *Marguerite Duras*. Paris: Albatros, 1976. Trans. Edith Cohen and Peter Connor. San Francisco: City Lights Books, 1987.

Duras, Marguerite, and Xavière Gauthier. *Les parleuses*. Paris: Editions de Minuit, 1974.

Duras, Marguerite, and Jérôme Beaujour. *La vie matérielle*. Paris:

P.O.L.: 1987
Fedkiw, Patricia. "Marguerite Duras: Feminine Field of Hysteria." *Enclitic* 6.2 (1982): 78–86.
Gauthier, Xavière. "Marguerite Duras et la lutte des femmes." *Magazine littéraire* 158 (mars 1980): 16–19.
Hulley, Katherine. "Contaminated Narratives: The Politics of Form and Subjectivity in Marguerite Duras's *The Lover*." *Discourse* 15.2 (Winter 1992–93): 30–50.
Husserl-Kapit, Susan. "An Interview with Marguerite Duras." *Signs* 1.2 (Winter 1975): 423–434.
Lydon, Mary. "L'Eden Cinéma: Aging and the Imagination in Marguerite Duras." *Memory and Desire: Aging—Literature—Psychoanalysis*. Ed. Kathleen Woodward and Murray M. Schwartz. Bloomington: Indiana University Press, 1986. 154–167.
———. "The Forgetfulness of Memory: Jacques Lacan, Marguerite Duras, and the Text." *Contemporary Literature* 29.3 (1988): 351–368.
Makward, Christiane. "Structures du silence/du délire: Marguerite Duras/Hélène Cixous." *Poétique* 35 (1978): 314–324.
Marini, Marcelle. *Territoires du féminin avec Marguerite Duras*. Paris: Editions de Minuit, 1977.
O'Neill, Kevin C. "Structures of Power in Duras's *Un Barrage contre le Pacifique*." *Rocky Mountain Review of Language and Literature* 45.1–2 (1991): 47–60.
Pagès, Irène. "*Moderato Cantabile*, *L'Amant* et le non-dit ou dans les trous du discours." *French Literature Series* 16 (1989): 141–148.
Ramsay, Raylene. "Autobiographical Fictions: Duras, Sarraute, Simon, Robbe-Grillet: Re-Writing History, Story, Self." *International Fiction Review* 18.1 (1991): 25–33.
Ricouart, Janine. *Ecriture féminine et violence: une étude de Marguerite Duras*. Birmingham: Summa Publications, 1991.
Schuster, Marilyn R. *Marguerite Duras Revisited*. Twayne's World Author's Series 840. New York: Twayne, 1993.
Selous, Trista. "Marguerite and the mountain." *Contemporary*

French fiction by women: Feminist Perspectives. Ed. Margaret Atack and Phil Powrie. Manchester and New York: Manchester University Press, 1990. 84-95.

——. *The Other Woman: Feminism and Femininity in the Work of Marguerite Duras.* New Haven: Yale University Press, 1988.

Stimpson, Catherine. "Marguerite Duras: A 'W/Ringer''s Remarks." *L'Esprit Créateur* 30.1 (Spring 1990): 15-18.

Went-Daoust, Yvette. "L'Ecriture au féminin singulier: *L'Amant* de Marguerite Duras." *French Literature Series* 16 (1989): 149-163.

Willis, Sharon. *Marguerite Duras: Writing on the Body.* Urbana and Chicago: University of Illinois Press, 1987.

Studies on Autobiography

Barker-Nunn, Jeanne. "Telling the mother's story: history and connection in the autobiographies of Maxine Hong Kingston and Kim Chernin." *Women's Studies* 14.1 (1987): 55-63.

Beaujour, Michel. *Miroirs d'encre: rhétorique de l'autoportrait.* Paris: Seuil, 1980.

Benstock, Shari, ed. *The Private Self: Theory and Practice of Women's Autobiographical Writings.* Chapel Hill and London: University of North Carolina Press, 1988.

Brée, Germaine. "Autogynography." *The Southern Review.* 22.2 (1986): 223-230.

——. "George Sand: The Fictions of Autobiography." *Nineteenth-Century French Studies* 4.4 (1976): 438-49.

Brodzki, Bella, and Celeste Schenck, eds. *Life/Lines: Theorizing Women's Autobiography.* Ithaca: Cornell University Press, 1988.

Bruss, Elizabeth W. *Autobiographical Acts: The Changing Situation of a Literary Genre.* Baltimore: Johns Hopkins University Press, 1976.

Chevigny, Bell Gale. "Daughters Writing: Toward a Theory of Women's Biography." *Feminist Studies* 9.1 (1983): 79-102.

Gilmore, Leigh. *Autobiographics: A Feminist Theory of Women's*

Self-Representation. Ithaca: Cornell University Press, 1994.
Gunn, Janet Varner. *Autobiography: Towards a Poetics of Experience.* Philadelphia: University of Pennsylvania Press, 1982.
Heilbrun, Carolyn G. *Writing a Woman's Life.* New York: W. W. Norton, 1988.
Hewitt, Leah D. *Autobiographical Tightropes.* Lincoln and London: University of Nebraska Press, 1990.
Jelinek, Estelle C., ed. *Women's Autobiography: Essays in Criticism.* Bloomington: Indiana University Press, 1980.
Lejeune, Philippe. *L'autobiographie en France.* Paris: A. Colin, 1971.
———. *Le pacte autobiographique.* Paris: Editions du Seuil, 1975.
Lionnet, Françoise. *Autobiographical Voices: Race, Gender, Self-Portraiture.* Ithaca: Cornell University Press, 1989.
Lorde, Audre. *Zami: a new spelling of my name.* Watertown, MA: Persephone, 1982.
Lury, Celia. "Reading the self: autobiography, gender and the institution of the literary." *Off-Centre: Feminism and cultural studies.* Ed. Sarah Franklin, Celia Lury, and Jackie Stacy. London: Harper Collins Academic, 1991. 97–108.
Man, Paul de. "Autobiography as De-facement." *Modern Language Notes* 94.5 (1979): 919–930.
Marcus, Laura. "Coming Out in Print: Women's Autobiographical Writings Revisited." *Prose Studies: History, Theory, Criticism* 10.1 (1987): 102–107.
Marks, Elaine. "The Dream of Love: A Study of Three Autobiographies." *The Twentieth-Century French Fictions: Essays for Germaine Brée.* Ed. Georges Stambolian. New Brunswick: Rutgers University Press, 1975. 73–88.
———. "'I Am My Own Heroine': Some Thoughts about Women and Autobiography in France." *Teaching about Women in the Foreign Languages.* Ed. Sidonie Cassirer. Old Westbury, N.Y.: The Feminist Press, 1975. 1–10.
Miller, Nancy K. "Autobiographical Deaths." *Massachusetts Review* 33.1 (Spring 1992): 19–47.

Morgan, Janice, and Colette T. Hall, eds. *Redefining Autobiography in Twentieth-Century Women's Fiction.* New York and London: Garland Publishing, 1991.
Neuman, Shirley. *Autobiography and Questions of Gender.* London: Frank Cass, 1991.
———. "'Your Past...Your Future': Autobiography and Mother's Bodies." *Genre—Trope—Gender.* Ed. Barry Rutland. Ottawa: Carleton University Press, 1992. 53–86.
O'Callaghan, Raylene L. "Reading Nathalie Sarraute's *Enfance*: Reflections on Critical Validity." *Romanic Review* 80.3 (1989): 445–461.
Olney, James, ed. *Autobiography: Essays Theoretical and Critical.* Princeton, NJ: Princeton University Press, 1980.
Peterson, Linda H. "Female Autobiographer, Narrative Duplicity." *Studies in the Literary Imagination* 23.2 (Fall 1990): 165–176.
Smith, Sidonie. "Construing Truths in Lying Mouths: Truthtelling in Women's Autobiography." *Studies in the Literary Imagination* 23.2 (Fall 1990): 145–163.
———. "The Impact of Critical Theory on the Study of Autobiography: Marginality, Gender, and Autobiographical Practice." *A/B: Auto/Biography Studies* 3.3 (1987): 1–12.
———. *A Poetics of Women's Autobiography: Marginality and the Fictions of Self-Representation.* Bloomington and Indianapolis: Indiana University Press, 1987.
———. *Subjectivity, Identity, and the Body: Women's Autobiographical Practices in the Twentieth Century.* Bloomington: Indiana University Press, 1993.
Stanton, Domna C. "Autogynography: The Case of Marie de Gournay's *Apologie pour celle qui escrit.*" *French Literature Series* 12 (1985):18–31.
———. *The Female Autograph: Theory and Practice of Autobiography from the Tenth to the Twentieth Century.* Chicago: University of Chicago, 1984.

Feminist Criticism

Abel, Elizabeth, Marianne Hirsch, and Elizabeth Langland, eds. *The Voyage In: Fictions of Female Development.* Hanover: University Press of New England, 1983.

Abel, Elizabeth, ed. *Writing and Sexual Difference.* Chicago: University of Chicago Press, 1982.

Badinter, Elisabeth. *L'amour en plus.* Paris: Flammarion, 1980.

Bassin, Donna, Margaret Honey, and Meryle Mahrer Kaplan, eds. *Representations of Motherhood.* New Haven: Yale University Press, 1994.

Berg, Elizabeth. "The Third Woman." *Diacritics* 12 (1982): 11–20.

Cixous, Hélène. "Le rire de la méduse." *L'Arc* 61 (1975): 39–54.

——. "Le sexe ou la tête." *Les Cahiers du GRIF* 13 (1976): 5–20.

Cixous, Hélène, Madeleine Gagnon, and Annie Leclerc, eds. *La venue à l'écriture.* Paris: Union Générale d'Editions, 10/18, 1977.

Cowie, Elizabeth. "Woman as Sign." *m/f* 1 (1978): 49–63.

Daly, Brenda O., and Maureen T. Reddy, eds. *Narrating Mothers: Theorizing Maternal Subjectivities.* Knoxville: University of Tennessee Press, 1991.

Davidson, Cathy N., and E. M. Broner, eds. *The Lost Tradition: Mothers and Daughters in Literature.* New York: Frederick Ungar Publishing, 1980.

Dejean, Joan, and Nancy K. Miller. *Displacements: Women, Tradition, Literatures in French.* Baltimore and London: Johns Hopkins University Press, 1991.

"L'Ecriture féminine." Special Issue. *Contemporary Literature* 24 (1983).

Eisenstein, Hester. *Contemporary Feminist Thought.* Boston: G. K. Hall, 1983.

Eisenstein, Hester, and Alice Jardine, eds. *The Future of Difference.* Boston: G. K. Hall, 1980. New Brunswick, New

Jersey: Rutgers University Press, 1985.

Evans, Martha Noel. *Masks of Tradition: Women and the Politics of Writing in Twentieth-Century France.* Ithaca: Cornell University Press, 1987.

"Feminist Readings: French Texts, American Contexts." Special Issue. *Yale French Studies* 62 (1981).

Fuss, Diana. *Essentially Speaking.* New York: Routledge, 1989.

Gardiner, Judith Kegan. "The New Motherhood." *North American Review* 263.3 (1978): 72–76.

———. "On Female Identity and Writing by Women." *Critical Inquiry* 8.2 (1981): 347–361.

Gilbert, Sandra M., and Susan Gubar. "'Forward into the Past': The Complex Female Affiliation Complex." *Historical Studies in Literary Criticism.* Ed. Jerome McGann. Madison: University of Wisconsin Press, 1985. 240–265.

Graulich, Melody. "Somebody Must Say These Things: An Essay for My Mother." *The Intimate Critique: Autobiographical Literary Criticism.* Ed. Diane P. Freedman, Olivia Frey, and Frances Murphy Zauhur. Durham and London: Duke University Press, 1993. 175–189.

Greene, Gayle, and Coppélia Kahn, eds. *Making a Difference: Feminist Literary Criticism.* London: Methuen, 1985.

Heath, Stephen. "Difference." *Screen* 19 (1978): 51–112.

Hirsch, Marianne, and Evelyn Fox Keller, eds. *Conflicts in Feminism.* New York and London: Routledge, 1990.

Jacobus, Mary. "Freud's Mnemonic: Women, Screen Memories, and Feminist Nostalgia." *Michigan Quarterly Review* 26.1 (1987): 117–139.

———. *Reading Woman: Essays in Feminist Criticism.* New York: Columbia University Press, 1986.

———. "The Difference of View." *Women Writing and Writing about Women.* Ed. Mary Jacobus. New York: Barnes & Noble, 1979. 10–21.

Kahane, Claire. "Questioning the Maternal Voice." *Genders* 3 (1988): 82–91.

Kahn, Coppélia. "Excavating 'Those Dim Minoan Regions':

Maternal Subtexts in Patriarchal Literature." *Diacritics* 12 (1982): 32–41.
Kaplan, E. Ann. *Motherhood and Representation in Literature and Film, 1830–1960*. New York: Routledge, 1989.
Lauretis, Teresa de, ed. *Feminist Studies/Critical Studies*. Bloomington: Indiana University Press, 1986.
Le Clézio, Marguerite. "Mother and Motherland: The Daughter's Quest for Origins." *Stanford French Review* 5.3 (Winter 1981): 381–389.
Marks, Elaine, and Isabelle de Courtivron, eds. *New French Feminisms: An Anthology*. New York: Schocken Books, 1981.
Marks, Elaine. "Women and Literature in France." *Signs: Journal of Women in Culture and Language* 3.4 (1978): 832–842.
McConnell-Ginet, Sally, ed. *Women and Language in Literature and Society*. New York: Praeger, 1980.
Miller, Nancy K. "D'une solitude à l'autre: vers un intertexte féminin." *The French Review* 54.6 (1981): 797–803.
———. *The Poetics of Gender*. New York: Columbia University Press, 1986.
———. "Rereading as a Woman: The Body in Practice." *Poetics Today* 6.1–2 (1985): 291–299.
———. *Subject to Change: Reading Feminist Writing*. New York: Columbia University Press, 1988.
Moi, Toril, ed. *French Feminist Thought: A Reader*. Oxford: Basil Blackwell, 1987.
———. *Sexual/Textual Politics: Feminist Literary Theory*. London: Methuen, 1985.
"Mothers and Daughters." Special Edition. *Frontiers: A Journal of Women's Studies* 3.2 (1978).
"Mothers and Daughters in Literature." Special Issue. *Women's Studies: An Interdisciplinary Journal* 6.2 (1979).
Rich, Adrienne. *Of Woman Born: Motherhood as Experience and Institution*. New York: Norton, 1976.
Rose, Jacqueline. "Femininity and its Discontents." *Feminist Review* 14 (June 1983): 5–21.
———. *Sexuality in the Field of Vision*. London: Verso, 1986.

Ruddick, Sara. "Maternal Thinking." *Feminist Studies* 6.2 (1980): 342–367.

Scheman, Naomi. "Missing Mothers/Desiring Daughters, Framing the Sight of Women." *Critical Inquiry* 15.1 (1988): 62–89.

Sellers, Susan. *Language and Sexual Difference.* New York: St. Martin's Press, 1991.

Showalter, Elaine, ed. *The New Feminist Criticism: Essays on Women, Literature, and Theory.* New York: Pantheon, 1985.

Suleiman, Susan Rubin, ed. *The Female Body in Western Culture: Contemporary Perspectives.* Cambridge, MA: Harvard University Press, 1986.

"Toward a Feminist Theory of Motherhood." Special Edition. *Feminist Studies* 4.2 (1978).

Weedon, Chris. *Feminist Practice and Poststructuralist Theory.* Oxford: Basil Blackwell, 1987.

Werlock, Abby H. P. "A Profusion of Women's Voices: Mothers and Daughters Redefining the Myths." *Mother Puzzles: Daughters and Mothers in Contemporary American Literature.* Ed. Mickey Pearlman. Westport, CT: Greenwood, 1989. 172–184.

Williams, Linda R. "Happy families? Feminist reproduction and matrilineal thought." *New Feminist Discourses: Critical Essays on Theories and Texts.* Ed. Isobel Armstrong. London: Routledge, 1992. 48–64.

Wittig, Monique. "The Category of Sex." *Feminist Issues* 2.2 (1982): 63–68.

——. "One is Not Born A Woman." *Feminist Issues* 1.2 (1981): 47–54.

Psychoanalytic Theory

Ainley, Alison. "The Ethics of Sexual Difference." *Abjection, Melancholia, and Love: The Work of Julia Kristeva.* Ed. John Fletcher and Andrew Benjamin. London: Routledge, 1990. 53–62.

Balint, Alice. "Love for the Mother and Mother Love." 1939.

Primary Love and Psycho-Analytic Technique. Ed. Michael Balint. New York: Liveright Publishing, 1965. 109–127.

Baruch, Elaine Hoffman, and Lucienne J. Serrano. *Women analyzing women.* New York: New York University Press, 1988.

Brennan, Teresa, ed. *Between Feminism and Psychoanalysis.* London: Routledge, 1989.

Bruneau, Marie-Florine. "Psychoanalysis and Its Abject: What Lurks Behind the Fear of the 'Mother.'" *Studies in Psychoanalytic Theory* 1.2 (Fall 1992): 24–38.

Buck, Claire. "'O Careless, Unspeakable Mother': Irigaray, H.D. and Maternal Origin." *Feminist Criticism: Theory and Practice.* Ed. Susan Sellers. Toronto: University of Toronto Press, 1991. 129–142.

Burke, Carolyn. "Irigaray through the looking glass." *Feminist Studies* 7.2 (1981): 288–306.

Chodorow, Nancy, and Susan Contratto. "The Fantasy of the Perfect Mother." *Rethinking the Family: Some Feminist Questions.* Ed. Barrie Thorne and Marilyn Yalom. New York and London: Longman, 1982. 54–75.

Chodorow, Nancy. *The Reproduction of Mothering.* Berkeley: University of California Press, 1978.

Dinnerstein, Dorothy. *The Mermaid and The Minotaur: Sexual Arrangements and Human Malaise.* New York: Harper Colophon, 1977.

Doane, Janice, and Devon Hodges. *From Klein to Kristeva: Psychoanalytic Feminism and the Search for the "Good Enough" Mother.* Ann Arbor: University of Michigan Press, 1992.

Edelstein, Marilyn. "Metaphor, Meta-Narrative, and Mater-Narrative in Kristeva's 'Stabat Mater.'" *Body/Text in Julia Kristeva: Religion, Women, and Psychoanalysis.* Ed. David R. Crownfield. Albany: State University of New York Press, 1992. 27–52.

Feldstein, Richard, and Judith Roof, eds. *Feminism and Psychoanalysis.* Ithaca: Cornell University Press, 1989.

Felman, Shoshana, ed. *Literature and Psychoanalysis*, special issue of *Yale French Studies* 55/6 (1977). Reissued by Johns Hopkins University Press, 1982.
———. *What Does a Woman Want? Reading and Sexual Difference.* Baltimore: Johns Hopkins University Press, 1993.
Féral, Josette. "Antigone or *The Irony of the Tribe.*" *Diacritics* 8.3 (Fall 1978): 2–14.
Freud, Sigmund. "Female Sexuality." 1931. *Collected Papers.* Vol. 5. Ed. James Strachey. London: Hogarth Press, 1950. 252–272.
———. "La féminité." 1933. *Nouvelles conférences sur la psychanalyse.* Paris: Gallimard Folio/Essais, 1984. 150–181.
———. "Mourning and Melancholia." 1917. *SE* vol. 14. 237–258.
———. "Some Psychical Consequences of the Anatomical Distinction between the Sexes." 1925. *SE* vol. 19. 243–258.
Gallop, Jane. *The Daughter's Seduction: Feminism and Psychoanalysis.* Ithaca: Cornell University Press, 1982.
———. *Reading Lacan.* Ithaca: Cornell University Press, 1985.
———. "Reading the Mother Tongue: Psychoanalytic Feminist Criticism." *Critical Inquiry* 13.2 (1987): 314–329.
———. *Thinking Through the Body.* New York: Columbia University Press, 1988.
Gardiner, Judith Kegan. "In the Name of the Mother: Feminism, Psychoanalysis, Methodology." *LIT: Literature—Interpretation—Theory* 1.4 (May 1990): 239–252.
Garner, Shirley Nelson, Claire Kahane, and Madelon Springnether, eds. *The (M)other Tongue: Essays in Feminist Psychoanalytic Interpretation.* Ithaca: Cornell University Press, 1985.
Hirsch, Marianne. "Maternal Anger: Silent Themes and Meaningful Digressions in Psychoanalytic Feminism." *Minnesota Review* 29 (1987): 81–87.
———. "Mothers and Daughters." *Signs* 7.1 (1981): 200–222.
———. *The Mother/Daughter Plot: Narrative, Psychoanalysis, Feminism.* Bloomington: Indiana University Press, 1989.
Holmlund, Christine. "The Lesbian, the Mother, the Heterosexual Lover: Irigaray's Recodings of Difference." *Feminist Studies*

17.2 (Summer 1991): 283–308.

Irigaray, Luce. *Ce sexe qui n'en est pas un.* Paris: Editions de Minuit, 1977.

———. *Et l'une ne bouge pas sans l'autre.* Paris: Editions de Minuit, 1979.

———. "La différence sexuelle." *Ethique de la différence sexuelle.* Paris: Editions de Minuit, 1984. 13–25.

———. *Le corps-à-corps avec la mère.* Montréal: Editions de la pleine lune, 1981.

———. *Speculum de l'autre femme.* Paris: Editions de Minuit, 1974.

Jardine, Alice. "Theories of the Feminine: Kristeva." *enclitic* 4 (1980): 5–16.

Klein, Melanie, and Joan Rivière. *Love, Hate and Reparation.* 1937. London: Hogarth, 1953.

Klein, Melanie. *The Selected Melanie Klein.* Ed. Juliet Mitchell. New York: Macmillan, 1987.

Kristeva, Julia. "L'abjet de l'amour." *Tel Quel* 91 (Spring 1982): 17–32.

———. "Approche de l'abjection." *Pouvoirs de l'horreur.* Paris: Editions du Seuil, 1980. 9–39.

———. *Desire in Language.* Ed. Leon S. Roudiez. Oxford: Blackwell; New York: Columbia University Press, 1980.

———. "Héréthique de l'amour." *Tel Quel* 74 (Winter 1977): 30–49.

———. *Histoires d'amour.* Paris: Denoël, 1983.

———. "Maternité selon Giovanni Bellini." *Polylogue.* Paris: Editions du Seuil, 1977. 409–435.

———. *La révolution du langage poétique.* Paris: Editions du Seuil, 1974.

———. *Soleil noir: dépression et mélancolie.* Paris: Gallimard, 1987.

Kuykendall, Eléanor H. "Toward an Ethic of Nurturance: Luce Irigaray on Mothering and Power." *Mothering: Essays in Feminist Theory.* Ed. Joyce Trebilcot. Totowa, NJ: Rowan and Allanheld, 1984. 263–274.

Lacan, Jacques. "L'instance de la lettre dans l'inconscient ou la raison depuis Freud." *Ecrits I*. Paris: Editions du Seuil, 1966. 249–289
——. "La signification du phallus." *Ecrits II*. Paris: Editions du Seuil, 1966. 685–95.
——. "Le stade du miroir comme formateur de la fonction du je." *Ecrits I*. Paris: Editions du Seuil, 1966. 89–97.
Lechte, John. *Julia Kristeva*. London: Routledge, 1990.
Millot, Catherine. "The Feminine Super-Ego. Together with Discussion by J. Mitchell, J. Rose, and Others." *m/f* 10 (1985): 21–38.
Mitchell, Juliet, and Jacqueline Rose, eds. *Feminine Sexuality: Jacques Lacan and the Ecole Freudienne*. New York: Norton, 1982.
Mitchell, Juliet. *Psychoanalysis and Feminism: Freud, Reich, Laing and Women*. New York: Random House, 1974.
Moi, Toril, ed. *The Kristeva Reader*. New York: Columbia University Press, 1986.
——. "Representation of Patriarchy: Sexuality and Epistemology in Freud's Dora." *Feminist Review* 9 (October 1981): 60–74.
Oliver, Kelly, ed. *Ethics, Politics, and Difference in Julia Kristeva's Writing*. New York and London: Routledge, 1993.
Plaza, Monique. "The Mother/The Same: Hatred of the Mother in Psychoanalysis." *Feminist Issues* 2.1 (1982): 75–99.
Pujade-Renaud, Claude. "La chimère maternelle et le sceau paternel." *Europe: Revue Littéraire Mensuelle* 631–632 (1981): 86–95.
Rivière, Joan. "Womanliness as Masquerade." *International Journal of Psycho-Analysis* 10 (1929): 303–313.
Sayers, Janet. "Feminism and Mothering: A Kleinian Perspective." *Women's Studies International Forum* 7.4 (1984): 237–241.
——. *Sexual Contradictions: Psychology, Psychoanalysis, and Feminism*. London: Tavistock, 1986.
Schor, Naomi. "This Essentialism Which is Not One: Coming to Grips With Irigaray." *Differences* 1.2 (1989): 38–58.
Sprengnether, Madelon. *The Spectral Mother: Freud, Feminism,*

and Psychoanalysis. Ithaca: Cornell University Press, 1990.
Strouse, Jean, ed. *Women and Analysis: Dialogues on Psychoanalytic Views of Femininity.* New York: Dell, 1974.
Swan, Jim. "*Mater* and Nannie: Freud's Two Mothers and the Discovery of the Oedipus Complex." *American Imago* 31 (1974): 1–64.
Whitford, Margaret, ed. *The Irigaray Reader.* Oxford: Basil Blackwell, 1991.
——. "Luce Irigaray and the Female Imaginary: Speaking as a Woman." *Radical Philosophy* 43 (1986): 3–8.
——. *Luce Irigaray: Philosophy in the Feminine.* London and New York: Routledge, 1991.
Wright, Elizabeth. *Psychoanalytic Criticism: Theory in Practice.* London and New York: Methuen, 1984.

General Reference

Laplanche, Jean, and J.-B. Pontalis. *Vocabulaire de la psychanalyse.* Paris: Presses Universitaires de France, 1967.
Petit Robert: dictionnaire alphabétique & analogique de la langue française. Ed. Paul Robert. Paris: Le Robert, 1982.
Shipley, Joseph T. *Dictionary of Word Origins.* New York: Philosophical Library, 1945.

Index

Abjection: in Beauvoir, 54–55, 57; in Duras, 77, 89–93, 135; in Kristeva, 8, 49–51
Agency: 118
Androcentrism: 2, 13, 47, 49, 68, 120
Ascher, Carol: 69n.1
Autobiography criticism: 115–21
Autogynography: 6, 121
Beauvoir, Simone de: *Le deuxième sexe*, 48; *Mémoires d'une jeune fille rangée*, 51–53, 56, 58, 60; *Une mort très douce*, 53–55, 59–65
Beggar women: 83–85, 88, 90–91, 106, 109, 112n.9
Benstock, Shari: 147n.2
Brodzki, Bella: 119, 127, 147n.2
Bruss, Elizabeth: 115
Castration: 30
Chester, Suzanne: 113n.16
Cixous, Hélène: 14–15, 43n.2
Cohen, Susan D.: 111n.2
Colette: *La maison de Claudine*, 21–23, 27, 31–33, 36; *La naissance du jour*, 23–26, 33–35; *Sido*, 26–28, 36–38
Condensation: 140
Demeter and Persephone: 28
"Difference": in Beauvoir, 67, 134; in Colette, 13–14, 129; in Duras, 139; in Irigaray, 76, 116; representation of, 6, 9, 115–22, 145–46
Duras, Marguerite: *L'amant*, 82–87, 95–102; *L'amant de la Chine du Nord*, 87–88, 102–7; *Un barrage contre le Pacifique*, 77–82, 93–95; *L'Eden Cinéma*, 110, 111nn.1, 7, 112n.10
Ecriture féminine: 14–15, 39, 76, 116
Eisinger, Erica Mendelson: 43n.1
Engenderment: 4, 120
Essentialism: 116–17
Evans, Mary: 69n.1
Family romance: 29, 36
Felman, Shoshana: 147n.3
"Feminine" genealogy: 15
"Feminine" identity: 5–6
"Femininity": in Beauvoir, 8–9, 45, 49, 57, 67, 68, 132–34; in Colette, 128; construction of, 7, 118, 143–44; in Duras, 137; in Freud, 118
Flieger, Jerry Aline: 10n.1, 43n.1, 43–4n.7
Fraiman, Susan D.: 43n.1
Freud, Sigmund: identification, 56–57; mother-daughter bond, 39, 53–54; "Mourning and Melancholia," 19; theorization of family, 1–2, 73–74
Gallop, Jane: 10n.1
Gilmore, Leigh: 147n.2

Hirsch, Marianne: 43nn.1, 4, 113n.16
Huffer, Lynne: 43nn.1, 6
Husserl-Kapit, Susan: 111n.4
Hysteria: 112n.9, 140, 143
Identification: in Beauvoir, 55, 56–57, 59–60, 64, 67, 134; in Duras, 75, 143; in Kristeva, 8, 51, 112n.8
Imaginary: 95
Incest taboo: 37
"Indifference": 70n.9, 75–76, 146
Introjection: 89–93
Irigaray, Luce: *Ce sexe qui n'en est pas un*, 8, 13, 24–25, 30; and Colette, 12–18, 38, 40; *Le corps-à-corps avec la mère*, 8, 11, 13, 15, 20–21, 28–29, 30, 40–41; *Et l'une ne bouge pas sans l'autre*, 8, 13, 20, 31, 76, 80, 82, 93, 95, 99; and specularity, 9; *Speculum de l'autre femme*, 13, 70n.9, 75
Jacobus, Mary: 69n.2
Jouissance: 29–30, 38, 141
Jouve, Nicole Ward: 44n.11
Klein, Melanie: 12
Kristeva, Julia: and Duras, 9; "Héréthique de l'amour," 66; *Histoires d'amour*, 8, 49, 51, 69n.7; mother-child relation, 116, 145; *Pouvoirs de l'horreur*, 8, 48, 49–51, 90; primary narcissism, 69n.7; *La révolution du langage poétique*, 69n.3; *Soleil noir: dépression et mélancolie*, 112n.8

Lacan, Jacques: desire, 26, 66; "L'instance de la lettre dans l'inconscient ou la raison depuis Freud," 147n.7; language, 74; "Le stade du miroir comme formateur de la fonction du je," 95
Laplanche, Jean: 57, 147n.6, 148n.8
Lastinger, Valérie: 43n.1
Law of the Father: in Colette, 41; in Kristeva, 77, 91–92; and personality formation, 4; and women, 117, 141, 142
Legend: 72–73
Lejeune, Philippe: 115
Lionnet, Françoise: 147n.2
Lorde, Audre: 111n.6
Lydon, Mary: 44n.9, 111n.2
Mantello, Elisabeth: 147n.1
Marini, Marcelle: 111n.5
Marks, Elaine: 43n.1, 44n.12, 69n.6
Maternal desire: 120, 142; in Beauvoir, 59; in Colette, 26, 32–34, 37–38; in Irigaray, 30; in Kristeva, 76, 91
Maternal madness: in *L'amant*, 72, 84–85, 92–93; in *L'amant de la Chine du Nord*, 88–89; in *Un barrage contre le Pacifique*, 82, 95; in Duras' work in general, 75, 86, 135, 137, 138
Materrenelle: 11
Matricide: 13, 17, 41, 82,

108–9, 110
McCarty, Mari Ward: 43n.1
Miller, Nancy, K.: 43nn.1, 6, 69n.4
Mirror: self-representation, 97, 107, 118; woman as, 97–98
Mirror phase: 49, 51, 95, 99, 102, 119
Mirroring, mother-daughter: in autobiography, 139, 144; in Irigaray, 9, 20, 31, 76, 99
Misogyny: and complicity, 47, 48, 143–144; and engenderment, 118, 120; and specularity, 95
Morgan, Janice: 111n.2
Mother as model: 4, 118, 120, 143; in Beauvoir, 46; in Colette, 6, 22, 29, 125
Name of the Father: 76–77
Neuman, Shirley: 147n.4
O'Brien, Mari H.: 147n.5
Oedipus complex: 12
O'Neill, Kevin C.: 112n.11
Other: in Beauvoir, 45, 46–47, 65, 66; in Lacan, 66; mother as, 143, 144; in Occidental culture, 51, 67, 147n.3
Palimpsest: 122–23, 126–29, 131, 136–39, 140, 145
Parler-femme: 13–14, 18, 116
Patriarchy: in Colette, 16, 28–29, 41; in Duras, 137; in Irigaray, 30; and language, 11, 117

Phallic mother: 21
Phallocentrism: 70n.9, 75
Pontalis, J.-B.: 57, 147n.6, 148n.8
Pre-oedipal: in Beauvoir, 55; in Colette, 12–13; and "difference," 142–43; feminist theorizations of, 13, 43n.4, 119–120; in Freud, 12; in Kristeva, 8, 49–51, 76–77
Ricouart, Janine: 113n.16
Schenck, Celeste: 147n.2
Schuster, Marilyn: 112n.12
Selous, Trista: 113n.15
Semiotic: 69n.3, 77, 91–92
Smith, Sidonie: 69n.5, 130, 143, 147n.2
Specula(riza)tion: 75–76, 106–7, 110; in *L'amant*, 98–99, 112–13n.14; in *L'amant de la Chine du Nord*, 102–103; in *Un barrage contre le Pacifique*, 94–95
Stanton, Domna: 5–6, 43n.2, 121, 147n.2
Symbolic: 69n.3, 77, 91–92, 100
Tinter, Sylvie: 43n.1
Unconscious: 73
Victimization: 4; in Beauvoir, 57, 60, 63; in Duras, 83, 88–89, 107–8, 110, 137
Weir, Allison: 112n.8
Willis, Sharon: 111n.3, 112n.9